D1445333

LIBERTY
IS DEAD.

**German
WCGStudies
Series**

WCGS German Studies Series

Wilfrid Laurier University Press and the Waterloo Centre for German Studies (WCGS) are pleased to announce a new book series in German Studies. The WCGS German Studies Series aims to publish two volumes per year in the fields of German applied linguistics, German cultural studies, history of German-speaking countries and peoples, German literature and film studies, German intellectual history, and theory. Senior editor John H. Smith (Diefenbaker Chair of German Literary Studies, University of Waterloo) and an editorial board of internationally recognized Germanists make this series a premier publishing venue in the discipline. We welcome submissions of both monographs and edited volumes that discuss original scholarly research of high quality.

Series Editor:
John H. Smith, Diefenbaker Chair of German Literary Studies,
University of Waterloo

For more information, please contact the WLU Press Acquisitions Editor:
Lisa Quinn
Acquisitions Editor
Wilfrid Laurier University Press
75 University Avenue West
Waterloo, ON N2L 3C5
Canada
Phone: 519-884-0710 ext. 2843
Fax: 519-725-1399
Email: quinn@press.wlu.ca

WILFRID LAURIER
UNIVERSITY PRESS

Margaret E. Derry, editor

LIBERTY
IS DEAD.

A Canadian in Germany, 1938

Wilfrid Laurier University Press acknowledges the support for this book from the Waterloo Centre for German Studies. We acknowledge the support of the Canada Council for the Arts for our publishing program. We acknowledge the financial support of the Government of Canada through the Canada Book Fund for our publishing activities.

Canada Council
for the Arts

Conseil des Art:
du Canada

ONTARIO ARTS COUNCIL
CONSEIL DES ARTS DE L'ONTARIO

Library and Archives Canada Cataloguing in Publication

Wegenast, Franklin W. (Franklin Wellington), 1876–1942
    Liberty is dead : a Canadian in Germany, 1938 / Margaret E. Derry, editor.

(WCGS German studies series)
Includes bibliographical references and index.
Also issued in electronic format.
ISBN 978-1-55458-053-8

    1. Wegenast, Franklin W. (Franklin Wellington), 1876–1942. 2. Wegenast, Franklin W. (Franklin Wellington), 1876–1942—Travel—Germany. 3. Wegenast, Franklin W. (Franklin Wellington), 1876–1942—Diaries. 4. Germany—History—1933–1945. 5. Germany—Description and travel. 6. German Canadians—Biography. 7. Lawyers—Canada—Biography. I. Derry, Margaret E. (Margaret Elsinor), 1945– II. Title. III. Series: WCGS German studies series (Waterloo, Ont.)

DD247.W43A3 2012   943.086092   C2011-907485-0

———

    Liberty is dead [electronic resource] : a Canadian in Germany, 1938 / Margaret E. Derry, editor.

Also issued in print format.
ISBN 978-1-55458-390-4 (PDF).—ISBN 978-1-55458-391-1 (EPUB)

    1. Wegenast, Franklin W. (Franklin Wellington), 1876–1942. 2. Wegenast, Franklin W. (Franklin Wellington), 1876–1942—Travel—Germany. 3. Wegenast, Franklin W. (Franklin Wellington), 1876–1942—Diaries. 4. Germany—History—1933–1945. 5. Germany—Description and travel. 6. German Canadians—Biography. 7. Lawyers—Canada—Biography. I. Derry, Margaret E. (Margaret Elsinor), 1945– II. Title. III. Series: WCGS German studies series (Waterloo, Ont. : Online)

DD247.W43A3 2012   943.086092   C2011-907486-9

RECYCLED
Paper made from
recycled material
FSC® C103567

Cover design by Blakeley Words+Pictures. Cover photo: Franklin Wegenast ca. 1938, from the Wegenast family collection. Text design by Blakeley Words+Pictures.

Every reasonable effort has been made to acquire permission for copyright material used in this text, and to acknowledge all such indebtedness accurately. Any errors and omissions called to the publisher's attention will be corrected in future printings.

This book is printed on FSC recycled paper and is certified Ecologo. It is made from 100% post-consumer fibre, processed chlorine free, and manufactured using biogas energy.

Printed in Canada

CONTENTS

LIST OF ILLUSTRATIONS

INTRODUCTION

I n February 1938, Adolf Hitler marched into Austria. At the same time a Canadian lawyer of German background was planning an extended trip to that troubled part of the world. Franklin Wellington Wegenast spent about four months over the spring and summer of 1938 in Europe. He took his car with him from Canada and drove from town to town, and country to country. Able to speak both German and French, he often stopped to talk to people along the way and offered rides to those requesting them. He listened to what his passengers had to say about their lives, the conditions they lived under, and their views on what was happening in Europe. He met distant German relatives. He heard Hitler speak in Innsbruck and so witnessed first-hand the escalating power of the National Socialist German Workers' Party (abbreviated as the NSDAP and known in English as the Nazi party) when Austria's independence crumbled.

Wegenast kept a diary of the trip, which today is composed of typed and handwritten pages. Worried about the European situation and deeply concerned about views he believed were commonly held by Germans, he gave a number of speeches, and wrote short articles for his local newspaper after he arrived home. (In surviving documents he spoke of both endeavours but did not provide information on where or when either occurred.) He was not able, however, to find a publisher interested in dealing with his manuscript as a whole. Even a few months could stale date information on Germany and Germans. Austria's fall in the spring of 1938, for example, was no longer news by late fall of that year. The problems now were the escalating racism in Germany after the Kristallnacht pogrom and the future of Czechoslovakia—and what next? Then, in 1939, war broke out. Wegenast died in 1942, leaving the diary in an unorganized state.

Today it provides first-hand impressions of Europe in the late 1930s from the perspective of a Canadian, and a German Canadian at that. Added information places the diary within a broader context. It helps, for example, to know something about the man who wrote it—that is, about his background and his interests. It is useful as well to learn what sort of contemporary information on Germany (and world affairs in relation to Germany) he would have been privy to before making the trip. It seems likely that such information would have shaped the views he expressed in the diary. It is important also to explain how Wegenast's diary fits into a rich literature on Germany in the 1930s.

Chapter 1 provides a biography of Franklin Wellington Wegenast. Although a third-generation German Canadian, his loyalty was to British Canada. After an early career in music—he taught singing and wrote music—he became a lawyer and went on to handle important cases such as the birth control trial of 1936.[1] Wegenast argued in front of the Privy Council several times. He was also the author of several books on Canadian law. His interests, broad and far-ranging, extended beyond the law and music. Wegenast pursued information about French architecture, the history of religion, and the background to Mennonite culture. He kept wild ducks and bred sheep. He had travelled throughout Europe many times before he made his trip in 1938, and he had located distant members of the Wegenast family in both Germany and Trieste, Italy. In 1938 he found some of them had Nazi sympathies.

Chapter 2 establishes the tenor of Canadian news reporting in the late 1930s, which would have influenced Wegenast's views concerning the German situation. He, like most citizens, would have had to rely on what the press (radio, newspaper, and magazines) had to say about events taking place and, more particularly, about German sentiment in relation to those events. Major American and British newspapers, the *New York Times* and the London *Times*, for example, had correspondents living in Germany, and their commentary was often picked up by Canadian newspapers. The *Globe* (*Globe and Mail* after 1936) commonly relied on this type of information.

From the diary it is certain that Wegenast read the London *Times* at least to a limited degree, and, like many Canadians, the *Globe and Mail*, Canada's major paper, regularly. I comment on underlying philosophies of Britain's major paper, the London *Times*, but provide more examples of remarks made by the *Globe and Mail* to illustrate (rather than analyze) how the German situation was handled by the press. The British *Times* did not always handle the German situation the same way the Canadian *Globe and Mail* did, even though the Canadian newspaper relied on reports of British foreign correspondents. The *Times* tended to favour more actively the policy of appeasement.[2] A brief review of the *Globe's* reporting from 1936 to early

1938 illustrates what sort of material was available to Canadians, and to Wegenast in particular. The actual wording of the *Globe and Mail*, rough and broken as it often was, shows how information bombarded readers, thereby creating a rising crescendo of fear. The tenor of the writing is as important as what was (accurately or inaccurately) stated as fact in the paper. In my brief review of the press's coverage, my main intention was to capture the tempo, the feeling, not to assess the accuracy of the commentary.

It was one thing for the papers to report on the unfolding of events; it was quite another to analyze why and how the events came about, or to assess German sentiment generally. Commentary addressing these issues was, therefore, somewhat rare in the *Globe*. Diplomats such as William E. Dodd (U.S. ambassador to Germany) expressed their impressions of Germany and this appeared in the Canadian press. A few well-known Canadians, Colonel George Drew being one, visited Germany. He wrote about his experiences, stating that Germans were well satisfied with Hitler. While Drew himself did not condone Hitler's activities, it was apparent to him that Germans did.[3] Trying to understand German attitudes toward Hitler and the Nazi party was complicated in the 1930s. A number of factors created that situation. To begin with, the state had effectively muzzled the country since 1933, and had furthermore begun monitoring sentiment, in order to find resistance to Hitler. Any real or even imagined opposition was actively repressed; therefore, people rarely wrote about their beliefs. They did not commonly confide in foreigners either. Germans themselves, let alone foreigners, found it difficult to assess correctly the general feeling of the people, as Victor Klemperer's diaries make clear.[4]

Chapter 3 reproduces Wegenast's diary, or journal. Life in Germany made him aware of threatening developments—developments so monolithic in nature that they were unlikely to be reversed. One had to actually hear and understand a Hitler speech, Wegenast found, to understand the implications behind the Nazi regime. When reading Wegenast's diary, which repeatedly emphasizes the dangers in Hitlerism, it is important to recognize that Hitler was by no means despised by everyone outside Germany. There was no open-and-shut case against the Führer or his administration. Former British Prime Minister David Lloyd George, for example, openly praised Hitler in the *Daily Express*—"the Washington of Germany," the saviour of his country, was the way Lloyd George described the Führer.[5] Esteem for Hitler could be found in Canada throughout the 1930s, even if evidence of this sentiment was not particularly apparent in the writings of major papers (pro-Hitler sentiment never openly appeared in the *Globe and Mail*). Prime Minister William Mackenzie King was favourably impressed with Hitler, for example.[6] Wegenast seemed to sense an undercurrent of support and respect for Hitler from various groups outside Germany as late as 1938.

Wegenast's journal also brings to life (or adds poignancy to) social and economic realities existing within the Third Reich. For example, he commented several times on how fascinated German children were with his North American car and how they often gathered around him to see it more closely or to hear the radio in it, and to talk to the Canadian. The ratio of cars to people in Germany was remarkably low compared to other countries in Europe and to North America, and no Volkswagen (or car of the people) reached Germans before 1945. The children's interest in Wegenast's vehicle (and subsequently in him) takes on a poignant meaning in that light. Wegenast later corresponded with one young lad, sending the child a picture of the car with the child standing beside it. The child, Hans Müller, wrote warmly in return. "I see that you, as a foreigner, have good memories of us, and that you liked our Fatherland," he said, and signed his letter "Heil Hitler."

The most complete version of the diary is the four-binder set of papers that Wegenast gave his law partner, Margaret Hyndman; yet even these do not contain all that he wrote. The material is in English (the few bits written in German I found that related to the diary—but were not actually in it— I had translated). Virtually all of the original manuscript is typed. A few loose handwritten pages have survived—again in English. The fact that most of the diary is typed suggests that Wegenast edited his handwritten entries. Some pages have only three lines on them, and many pages are not paginated. Handwritten comments on the side sometimes note which envelope the material belongs in—suggesting that Wegenast intended to do a lot more editorial work, and perhaps even break his collected information up under separate subject headings. He wrote the diary at different stages on his trip and mailed sections of it home to be typed, and to keep them safe. Once home he added material here and there, as a result of research or further contemplation of what he had seen in Europe. Since he was a published writer, he might well have intended to produce a series of articles that were unrelated to each other. This makes a lot of sense when looking at the design of the document as it stands today.

My editorial work was driven by several considerations. To begin with, I used the diary to describe Nazi Germany and attitudes of Germans and other Europeans to the situation. Because the diary is a loosely constructed document, it acts as a repository of collected information on various subjects that are not necessarily related to each other or to German issues. I included all passages—in any version that I had—that concerned Germany. I added existing correspondence—that is, the pitifully little that has survived. While

I removed most of the material on his ship voyage, I included the part about the costume party because I thought this section described something of the nature of the man. I left out Wegenast's impressions of Gibraltar and Marseilles—places that the ship visited. Wegenast disembarked at Naples, and his remarks on his travels through Italy compose the largest section that I removed. He did not say much about fascism here. Most of the photos that he took have not survived, and the ones that have are not particularly interesting. I did not include them.

I also edited quite severely his work on Mennonites. He wrote about genealogy and traced North American families he knew back to the European Mennonites he met in his travels. Wegenast spoke to Mennonites in Luxembourg, France, Germany, and Switzerland, on whom he must have kept separate notes, not included in the diary. His deep interest in French cathedral architecture led to many observations made on the subject, the volume of which I reduced for this book.

Because I wanted the diary to read in an interesting way, I tried to avoid repetitious comments and extraneous descriptions of things that were not interesting. It had to be a story that flowed. This type of editing meant the removal of the odd sentence in the middle of passages, and also of short paragraphs here and there. For example, Wegenast translated a section from a magazine on the history of Sulz, but this seemed too touristy in orientation to warrant inclusion. I also left out his general comments on various branches of the Wegenast family—he asked about a number of them while near Sulz. In order to make the story flow, I added short sections to connect the entries. I corrected spelling, too, in order to make the diary a smoother read. There are some exceptions, however, most notably the spelling of "führer," which I left as "fuehrer" in the diary text and in newspaper quotations. Typing at that time did not account for the "ü." Any text in square brackets within a quotation has been added by me.

I made sure that Wegenast's voice came through. I was careful, therefore, not to edit terms that could be considered offensive, such as "wops" and the like, and the sometimes extremely anti-German sentiment (although this always seemed conflicted with an underlying warmth and respect). I believed I would be falsifying his thoughts if I left these views out. It would have been easy to do so, and that fact made me see how critical it is to edit a diary with honesty. I tried as well to leave in enough stories and descriptions to illustrate how broad ranging his interests were; to give a sense of the person. Wegenast seemed to be an obsessive sort of man. In order to be true to my writer, I left in his obsessions—or overkill as the case may be. He was opinionated, it appears, but that helps to explain the acuteness of his some of his observations. A startlingly honest person, Wegenast often criticized himself as much as others.

Chapter 4 looks at Wegenast's correspondence with a young German between December 1938 and early 1939 (after Wegenast had returned home) that reveals even more clearly what the trip had taught him. The intensity of his feelings, his fear for the future, and his conviction that a collision course was in store for the world are powerfully evident in the letters and notes. Here he made some of his clearest statements on how he viewed history, politics, and society generally and with respect to developments in Germany and the nature of German thinking. Here too we see what had become for him an obsessive and debilitating concern with the German situation.

Chapter 5 gives an overview of Wegenast's impressions, and does so within the framework of contemporary private views and modern scholarship. There has been a considerable outpouring of material on Germany and Germans over the last twenty years—both newly published primary source documents (including diaries such as that by Victor Klemperer[7]—a particularly significant one) and secondary scholarly material (the combined work of R. Evans and I. Kershaw[8] being of special value to someone who reads only in English). The diary should be seen within that framework. While it could be analyzed against scholarly material in considerable detail, this book points out only the major ways Wegenast's thinking relates to that of modern specialists in the area of German history. My intention was to provide contextualization for the diary by introducing information arising from such sources. A comprehensive treatment of material on Germany in the 1930s is beyond the scope of this book, but if the reader wishes to know more about Germany and German views (or specific issues within that framework), the selected bibliography at the end of this work will provide a good starting point into the general field.

Because Wegenast spoke as an outsider, this diary fits most succinctly within the genre of travel literature of foreigners to Germany in the 1930s, a relatively new source studied by scholars in attempts to understand life in the Reich and German points of view. As O. Lubrich wrote in the introduction to *Travels in the Reich, 1933–1945*:

Reports by foreign visitors open up new perspectives on European history. They contribute to the historiography of the Third Reich by focusing on everyday life from different angles and with different approaches. Because they register the reality of life in Nazi Germany through the eyes of an outsider; they report it in a different way than contemporary German witnesses have portrayed it. And, in a narrower sense, they reveal why, and in what circumstances, foreigners traveled in Germany and how they were able to experience the country.[9]

All travel literature is multi-layered in meaning and rich in information. Both the sameness and the variation of opinions provide an interwoven and complex tapestry of insight into the nature of the Reich. Wegenast's journal fits into that genre, but it also provides a window into Canadian and North American thinking about conditions in Europe that did not arise from a reporter or diplomat perspective.

The route that Wegenast followed while collecting stories about Germany can be outlined as follows. He travelled north through Italy, and thence east to Trieste. Next he headed north and west toward Austria. He stopped at Bolzano, an Italian town directly south of Innsbruck, and crossed into Austria. From Innsbruck he headed due west toward the Swiss and German border along Lake Constance. He entered Germany, passing through various towns such as Tuttlington, Rottweil, and Sulz-am-Neckar in Baden-Württemberg. From there, he headed for France. He was anxious for a break from Germany, and he wanted time to safely write up his impressions. Wegenast stayed at Strasbourg in Alsace, France. He then moved up along the French border, turning west to visit Reims. After seeing Reims, he headed north and slightly east, entering the Duchy of Luxembourg. Here he met and talked to a German Mennonite family. He then turned east and started on his way back into Germany, intending to speak to a number of other Mennonites, many of whom lived in the Rhineland-Palatinate area.

He crossed near Echternach and immediately was struck again by the difference in atmosphere between Germany and the bordering countries. He stayed with various Mennonite farmers and took in the spa at Bad Nauheim, where he became interested in the medical effects of the waters. Here he also bought and read Rosenberg's *Myth of the Twentieth Century*.[10] Its focus on racial purity appalled Wegenast. He viewed the idea of racial purity as nonsense. He went on to Heidelberg. After doing more Mennonite research in various towns in the Rhineland-Palatinate and Baden-Württemberg area, he thankfully retreated into France at Wissembourg. While in Wissembourg and later in Geneva, Switzerland, he spent considerable time trying to analyze what he had experienced in Germany. While the diary covers the trip from late February until July, extracts relating specifically to German affairs were recorded in the period between mid-March and early June 1938.

FRANKLIN WELLINGTON WEGENAST, 1876–1942

1

Franklin Wellington Wegenast was born in the town of Waterloo, Waterloo County, Ontario, in June 1876. He was the oldest surviving child of Martin S. Wegenast and his wife, Dinah Sauer. The family was entirely of German descent, but Franklin's parents were both born in North America and raised in Waterloo County, which had been settled primarily by Germans between 1800 and 1850, emanating from two separate sources.

The first wave of German people coming to the county arrived from the United States, primarily from Pennsylvania. They belonged to various splinter religious sects and were known as Pennsylvania Dutch. Most were poor farmers who moved into Upper Canada after the American Revolution in order to preserve their religious way of life. In the 1830s a second wave of immigration began, this one from Germany. While many of these new Germans were Mennonite and Amish, most were either Lutheran or Catholic. The county's towns of Berlin (later Kitchener), Waterloo, and Preston grew quickly between 1848 and 1876 (the year Franklin was born) as a result of these immigration waves. People tended to speak German (or the Pennsylvania Dutch dialect of the language) in the home and in business, but the schools quickly adopted English as the language of education. Ties with both Germany and the United States remained strong throughout the nineteenth century, especially from a cultural standpoint. German interest in music played an important role in the county, and bands were formed as early as 1839. Singing festivals would draw people from miles around. Religion bound many to the United States. In 1836 a missionary was sent up from Pennsylvania to teach evangelicalism. A church was established in 1839. There was also a great deal of cross migration between this area and the United States by people of Pennsylvania Dutch background.[1]

Franklin's background reflected this dual German heritage and cultural inclination. His father, Martin, was a product of the second German migration to Waterloo. He was born in Waterloo County in 1836 to German parents who had arrived in the New World in 1833 from Holzhausen, Baden-Württemburg, with three children in tow. A wood mechanic, Martin had three daughters from a previous marriage before he married Dinah Sauer in 1874. Dinah had complicated connections to the Pennsylvania Dutch culture through both her mother (whose family had come to Canada from Pennsylvania), and her father, William Henry Sauer, who (after arriving from Bavaria) took to the religion of the Pennsylvania Dutch Evangelical mission. He became the first Canadian Evangelical preacher. By the age of ten, Dinah led the hymns sung in her father's church. Following the German custom of the times, singing was to be a large part of her life.

Franklin, then, grew up in a German household with strong cultural German roots and with religious ties to the Pennsylvania Dutch religion. It is probable that the language spoken in the home was the Pennsylvania Dutch dialect, but Franklin would have been aware of the different forms of German speaking. Perhaps that explains why he had a lifelong interest in languages. From his early years, he was involved with music, playing in a band as a young boy, and in adulthood turning to singing.[2]

Franklin supported himself from the age of twelve, and also managed to graduate from Kitchener high school at a time when few in the county went on to that form of higher education. At one point he boarded with an Amish family, and this experience in conjunction with his own religious background encouraged an interest in the historical development of the various sectors of the Mennonite religion. His family followed the religious path of his mother, Dinah—they were Evangelical. Martin's religion before his marriage to Dinah is not known. His immigration status suggests Lutheran more than Mennonite. It is interesting that Franklin would ultimately change his religious affiliation; as an adult he was Anglican. Perhaps this shift represented an early deliberate desire to shed his German background. There is no documentation to confirm this statement, but the change did fit with his increasing sense of Britishness. An interest in Evangelicalism, however, and indeed in all aspects of Christianity would stay with him all his life.

Franklin obtained a teacher's certificate and at the age of eighteen launched himself as a public school teacher. By 1898 Wegenast was teaching school in Colchester South, Essex County, and studying music more seriously with the view of making this his profession. He formed music classes and ran concerts in the area. It was at one of these that he was introduced to his future wife, Margaret Mary Bell, born in August 1878. Margaret's family

Franklin Wegenast as a boy, playing in a band (date unknown). His interest in and love of music became a part of his life at an early age. (Wegenast family papers, private collection)

background—she was of Scottish descent—encouraged a shedding of his German cultural heritage.[3] It was music, however, that drew Franklin and Margaret together. Margaret played the violin in Wegenast's concerts. In August 1901 they married at the farm "Nuttwood" and took up residence in the town of Simcoe, where Wegenast had moved in 1900. Here he taught music in the public schools, ran a business of singing lessons, and organized concerts. He was also choirmaster of the Presbyterian church in Simcoe. He earned almost as much from his music as from teaching. In 1900, for example (according to the Canada Census of 1901), he earned $500 teaching in the public school, and $400 from his musical endeavours. Wegenast took his music seriously and began to prepare for the A.T.C.M. Associate degree in singing from the Royal Conservatory of Music in Toronto.[4] At the same time he mastered the tonic sol-fa system of music, and came to appreciate the philosophy, beauty, and art of the system, as well as its value in teaching music.

Wegenast decided later that year to move to Woodstock, where better opportunities for teaching music existed. Wegenast became choirmaster

Franklin Wegenast as a young man, date unknown. (Wegenast family papers, private collection)

of the Central Methodist Church in Woodstock, and at the same time graduated with an associate certificate from the Royal Conservatory of Music with honours.

Unsatisfied with what he was doing, and seeking what seemed to him greater fulfillment, he became interested in studying the law and articled with the lawyer John Soper McKay.[5] Fully committed to the law at this point, Wegenast moved in late 1905 to Brampton in Peel County, which was near enough to Toronto that he could commute for courses in law at Osgoode Hall. In order to support himself and his wife, Franklin took a job as choirmaster of the Brampton Presbyterian Church. His salary was set at $1,200 a year. In 1906 and 1907 he was conductor of the Brampton Choral Society, and he wrote music as well. Margaret often accompanied him when he sang. In October 1906 his only surviving child, Elsinor Louise, was born.

Wegenast graduated from law school in 1909, having won the Christopher Robinson Memorial prize. (Later he took the exams for an L.L.B. at the University of Toronto and passed with first class honours.)[6] He went into the law office of B.F. Justin for four months, practised on his own for the same length of time, and then became counsel for the Canadian Manufacturer's' Association, organizing its first legal department. During the seven years he was with the Association he appeared in a series of

Franklin and Margaret Wegenast with their only surviving child, Elsinor Louise, 1907. Franklin and Margaret had four other babies that died within a few days of birth. (Wegenast family papers, private collection)

cases involving constitutional law and rights of the Dominion and provincial governments. Wegenast also represented the CMA during a three-year investigation before Sir William Meredith[7] and subsequently prepared a draft of the Workman's Compensation Act for Ontario. In 1911 he was called to the bar of Manitoba and wrote a pamphlet, *Workmen's Compensation for Injuries*, being a "sketch of the present law in Ontario and a comparison of the systems of some other countries." He also published a book, *Extraprovincial Corporations*. He prepared draft acts for Nova Scotia and New Brunswick, and the Compensation Acts of these and other provinces were for the most part, based on drafts prepared by Wegenast.

During this time he opened a law office at 67 Yonge Street in Toronto and continued to practise law in Brampton as well. Wegenast also involved himself in local politics. He sat on the town council in 1909, was reeve in 1923 and 1924 and, subsequently, mayor from 1925–28 and again in 1940. Wegenast beautified the southern entrance to the business section of the town, by straightening the way the creek ran through and building retaining walls for it. He loved landscape gardening and kept sheep, ducks, and horses on his Brampton property, which was composed of 25 acres of land and two old barns on Highway 10 (Main Street). Over the years, chickens, a dog, rabbits, and many cats also lived there. (His deep interest in the land and in farm animals would resurface in his observations of the French and German countryside.) While he had less time for music (he resigned from his position at the Brampton Presbyterian Church choir in 1915), he still managed to sing at some concerts. (As late as 1940 he sang solo at the Presbyterian Church.)

His work with the Canadian Manufacturers' Association took him to London, England, to argue in front of the Privy Council, the first time being in 1914 for the John Deere Plough Company case. His wife and daughter went with him but returned to Canada when war broke out. Wegenast stayed on, hoping to help with the war effort because of his ability to speak German. He had planned to go to Germany to seek out distant relatives after completing his legal work in Britain, but the war prevented this. In spite of his German background, he was thoroughly Canadian, and British Canadian in his outlook by this time. His interest in and practice of law, and his marriage into a Scottish Canadian family only increased his orientation toward Britain and away from his German roots. By this time both his parents had died, his mother in 1913, and his father in 1914. (One wonders what these German people would have thought of the situation in the Western world.)

In 1920 he was in London again on a Privy Council case, and wrote home to his wife, Margaret, about life in England. He promised to send her newspapers he had read and also brochures to any theatre that he went to.

In late November, he found the hotels horrifyingly cold in London and in the towns he visited outside that city. "There were several inches of snow and snowed some more during the night," Wegenast wrote. "Imagine our house in Brampton in such weather without any fire at all. And that is England." He wondered about the wisdom of trying to visit Scotland in the "beastly climate." "Even 1st class coaches not heated," he added. "Awful hotels." Wegenast may have considered himself British in orientation, but these comments suggest that in fact he was thoroughly Canadian.

He was fascinated by changes in dress he saw in England compared to before the war. "London is different in some ways," he explained to Margaret, "Oh so different from five years ago when things were dark for us. But there are differences from the older and more prosperous times. I saw only three silk hats [on men] in all London this forenoon." Alterations in women's clothing were more remarkable. The shoes they wore he found attractive, but he was not so sure about other aspects of apparel. "The skirts!" he said. "They are rather beating the Americans to it in the matter of shortness. And I have seen some very daring creations by way of evening dresses."[8] Women and style seemed to be of considerable interest to him and he would take note of feminine dress while in France and Germany in 1938.

In 1921, after his work with the Privy Council was done, Wegenast went on to France and thence to Germany. He wanted to know more about his heritage. He visited Stuttgart, Sulz-am-Neckar, and Holzhausen in Baden-Württemberg, looking for Wegenast family members who had been separated for at least three generations. He felt at home in Germany and found it easy to communicate with everyone. He talked to everyone he met. Except for a few confrontations over the past war, which Wegenast avoided being drawn into, he felt in accord with Germans.[9]

In the fall of 1922 it was planned that his wife and daughter, Elsinor, spend the year in England, and join him while he took another case to the Privy Council. Wegenast was unable to leave as early as he had hoped because the case was delayed. His wife and daughter went on ahead of him. Elsinor was enrolled in school in England for two terms. Subsequently her mother took her to Paris where the two of them boarded with a French family and Elsinor went to a day school with the family's daughter. At last Wegenast arrived in England to argue in front of the Privy Council. Elsinor was left in Paris while Margaret and Franklin took a trip to Belgium and Germany. Their daughter joined them later in England. The family was together in England the summer of 1923, and in July, King George V and Queen Mary invited them to a garden party at Buckingham Palace. Social activities of this sort did not seem to make Wegenast less interested in common people, as his diary revealed. While openly proud of his success as a lawyer and of his British connection, he never came to see himself as someone detached from those of a lower social ranking.

During the winter that Margaret and Elsinor were away, Franklin continued with his law practice and also focused more on a project that he had had under way since roughly 1915, namely, the writing of his book on company law.[10] Margaret Hyndman, a young woman who had joined his law firm in 1920, worked with him on the project. Her deep interest in this undertaking would draw him into a close intellectual and mutually respectful relationship with her.[11] Wegenast's support of a young woman lawyer was unusual at the time. Women were rare in the legal profession, and the few that entered the law found it difficult to practise. His respect for Hyndman illustrated his deep commitment to the advancement of women in education, business, and the professions. Wegenast encouraged his only child, Elsinor, to pursue a higher education, which she ultimately did. After graduating from the University of Toronto in 1929 with a gold medal, Elsinor entered law school and graduated from Osgoode in 1933.

The years after his company law book was published, the 1930s, were especially rich for Wegenast intellectually and professionally. He plunged himself into the pursuit of knowledge in a variety of ways. A linguist who spoke German and French as well as English, he began to study Italian, and then Chinese.[12] Able to speak Gaelic like a native, many people in Brampton took him to be a Highlander. He did research into the historical background of the various religious sects that composed the Mennonite movement.[13] His legal career also commanded a great deal of his attention, and he was made King's Counsel in 1935 at a time when the title carried considerable prestige.

One of his clients was A.R. Kaufman, a descendent of Swiss Mennonites who had settled in Waterloo County in the mid-nineteenth century. Alvin Ratz Kaufman became involved in the rubber industry through his father, and in about 1906 formed the Kaufman Rubber Company. Perhaps their common German/evangelical religious backgrounds formed a bond that led to Kaufman hiring Wegenast as the company's lawyer, even though Wegenast had left the county years before the Kaufman Rubber Company was founded. At any rate the Toronto- and Brampton-based lawyer, and his assistant, Margaret Hyndman, came to look after the company's corporate affairs. Philanthropically inclined, Kaufman gave handsomely to local charities.[14] His involvement with social issues ultimately drew Wegenast into them.

In 1936 Wegenast, through Kaufman, became embroiled in the Dorothea Palmer trial, or the famous birth control case.[15] The trial brought Wegenast into the world of eugenics, and with contraception and its medical, ethical, and social implications. Franklin had not wanted to be legal counsel on the case—he had no interest in the contraceptive campaigns of the time, or in the underlying eugenic sterilization movements often attached to the birth control issue. Wegenast stated that he was not prepared to deal in court with the subject of birth control. In the 1970s and near the end of his life, Kaufman claimed that he had to convince Wegenast, said to be in poor health, to take the case on.[16] Hyndman, in her taped interviews from 1983 remarked, "Mr. Wegenast was interested in all [Kaufman's] business and legal problems, but when Mr. Kaufman started to talk about birth control he hardly listened to him, he thought it was just a fad of his." Margaret Hyndman was interested herself in the case and did some legal research before discussing the issue with Franklin. "I told him about [my research]," she added, "well he began to take an interest in it, you see, it was a real legal question then."[17] Having agreed to take on the case, Wegenast gave his best efforts to winning for the birth control cause.[18] Wegenast's interest in the legal questions around birth control was soon linked with his inherent concern for the rights of women. He quickly came to see birth control as central to women's ability to have control over their bodies. For him, birth control was an issue of personal freedom for women.

The background to the trial was as follows. With the depression of 1929, Kaufman had been forced to let workers in the company go, and through a company nurse he learned of the family situation common to many of his employees. She informed Kaufman that the poorest families often had the most children and that fact caused great financial hardship. She also implied that many of these families were limited intellectually. Kaufman became interested in the whole issue of birth control and founded the Parents' Information Bureau in 1930.[19] The bureau sent out agents, paid $1.50 per visit, to homes and offered information on birth control. If requested by the (married) women interviewed, the agents supplied condoms and spermicidal jellies at cost price. The bureau's service spread outside of Kitchener, and by 1936 Dorothea Palmer, a young woman hired by the organization, was canvassing Eastview, a small French-Canadian town in the Ottawa Valley, to see which married women wanted contraceptive information. On a second visit to a particular house, the police were waiting and arrested her under the Criminal Code on the basis that she was advertising and selling contraceptive devices. Kaufman was enraged, and prepared to fight the case in court with all his resources. The story of the Dorothea Palmer trial is complicated by the personality of A.R. Kaufman and his role in the birth control movement, which was not simply driven by concern for women having the right to control their bodies.[20]

Kaufman was concerned with over-propagation of the poor and the power of the Catholic Church, and he harboured anti-French-Canadian sentiment. He was particularly angry at the resistance that the Catholic Church put up against the work of his Parents' Information Bureau, and when Dorothea Palmer was arrested he believed this resulted from the instigation and planning of the church to bring the issue to a head.[21] One of his lifelong passions became sterilization of the defective. Kaufman argued that, even with contraception, from 5 to 10 per cent of the population should be sterilized. He wanted funds to support eugenic sterilization, and his aggressive anti-Catholicism led him to respond to papal attacks on sterilization by saying that cathedral choirs of male sopranos were composed of sterilized males. Mental deficiency was not the only form of defectiveness that concerned Kaufman. He believed that anyone suffering from tuberculosis, epilepsy, syphilis, nerve diseases, heart conditions, kidney conditions, congenital deafness, or congenital blindness qualified as defective and should be operated on. Kaufman was one of the founding members and main supporters of the Eugenics Society of Canada, which was formed in 1930.[22]

Scholars have noted that F.W. Wegenast became a member of the Eugenics Society and therefore conclude that it was shared eugenic interests that underlay the way that Wegenast handled the case—despite the fact that originally he had not wanted to be involved with the issue of birth control at any level. His lifelong interest in the rights of women suggested his concerns with birth control dovetailed with that issue. Even though it is usually admitted that Wegenast tended to stress such issues as the immorality of depriving individuals of contraceptive information, the right of women to control their reproduction, and the legitimacy of non-procreative sexual pleasure in his arguments before the court, it has been argued that Kaufman and Wegenast both had eugenic agendas.[23] Legal arguments set out in court, it has been stated, were "all subsumed under the broader argument that birth control would serve eugenic goals in subjecting reproduction to rational controls."[24] Evidence suggests, from the Dorothea Palmer Collection of documents, that Franklin learned about the eugenics movement as a result of the trial. It was not the other way around.

The archival holdings in the University of Waterloo of papers relating to the Dorothea Palmer trial are the records of Franklin Wellington Wegenast. Margaret Hyndman sent the files to Kaufman after Wegenast's death in 1942, and Kaufman subsequently gave them to the university. Wegenast organized his information to prove that birth control was "pro bono publico," or for the public good. While he tended to focus on the basis of liberty and the right of a woman to control her body, Wegenast set out his presentation under five headings—economic, eugenic, sociological, medical, and moral. He was prepared to use the general eugenic thinking of the time to support his argument that birth control was in the public interest. In other words, he was appealing to other people's beliefs, or explaining the "public good" in language they could understand.[25] Wegenast's involvement with the movement as a result of the trial, however, takes on considerable significance when considered in relation to what he would encounter in Germany with respect to eugenics.

Not long after the trial, Wegenast suffered a heart attack and in the spring of 1938 Kaufman funded a rest trip for Franklin in Europe. Wegenast wanted time to think, to relax, to explore, and to see again familiar sites that he knew well from earlier trips.

He kept a journal, which he began with the following introductory comments. "In the spring of 1938, obeying the advice of physicians, I spent several months loafing in Europe, preceded by a few days in Egypt, Palestine, and Greece. Instead of writing letters, I made pencil observations on pads of paper. These I sent in instalments from time to time to the office to have typewritten copies made for persons who might be interested,

A Portrait of Franklin Wegenast, taken at about the time he took the 1938 trip to Europe. (Wegenast family papers, private collection)

including myself." Wegenast returned home in July 1938. Just before war broke out, he took up a short but ultimately abortive correspondence with a young German named Sigfrid Schmidt, whom he had met in Reims, France. When Wegenast tried to work out his thoughts on Germany and German approaches to the world before writing to Sigfrid, who was an ardent supporter of the Nazi party and of Hitler, he became increasingly disenchanted with the idea of even communicating with this young man. And then war came. Wegenast's law practice suffered because of his German background. This situation is somewhat ironic given his intense Canadianism, his love of Britain, and his disgust with German sentiments of the times. He was one of the thousands of North American Germans who experienced discrimination during the war. In late May 1942 he went back to his old haunts in Waterloo County for a rest at Preston Springs hotel. Several days later Wegenast died there of kidney failure, probably aggravated by the continuing hypertension, which had led to his heart attack and which he had sought to learn more about while in Bad Nauheim.

After the end of the war, his three sisters (Ida, Sarah, and Elizabeth) corresponded with the German relatives he had met in 1921 and 1938, and provided clothing to them in the desperate times that followed 1945 in Germany. Drawings of the size of a child's foot were often included in these letters from Germany to help the Canadian sisters locate what was needed. Many of the letters expressed gratitude and appreciation for the kindness and generosity extended by the three Canadian women. The sisters were far from well-to-do. Their outpouring of help seems strange, not just for that reason but for others as well. Wegenast had been appalled at the pro-Hitler sentiment evident in some of these German relatives, a fact his sisters certainly would have known. One sister, Ida, had actively supported the Canadian war effort by working as a translator in Ottawa. These patriotic Canadian women found it in their hearts, above and beyond offensive German ideology and patriotism to their own country during wartime, to give to those so obviously in need after defeat. By the 1960s no one in their family could read the yellowing letters that the three women had preserved, because no one by that time could speak or read German. After a few efforts at translation, the letters were thrown out. The last connections with Germany that the Wegenast family had had vanished.

NEWSPAPER INFORMATION IN THE 1930S ON GERMANS AND THE GERMAN SITUATION

2

Wegenast's journal should be read with consideration of what he, a Canadian at home, read in the news about Germans and German sentiment in the late 1930s. News reporting and particularly the tenor of that reporting must have shaped his views before he took the trip, and he probably judged his experiences in Europe against what he had learned in Canada. It seems likely that Wegenast's perceptions about contemporary events and Germans arose primarily from what the media had to tell him, and not from direct communication with relatives in Germany. There is no evidence that Wegenast kept up regular correspondence with family members living in Germany after 1921 or, therefore, that he was affected by their opinions. How well could he, before his visit to Germany in 1938, understand what ordinary Germans thought? What sort of information was available to Canadians concerning Germans and Germany at that time and how was it presented? Central to the dispersion of news were the newspapers. It makes sense, then, to review the tenor of newspaper reporting that was available to him.

From comments made in the diary, it is clear that Wegenast read the *Globe* (after 1936 the *Globe and Mail*), published in Toronto. He also read, if not with great regularity, the *Times*, published in London, England. He may well have looked at other papers, but if so, they are unknown. I concentrate, therefore, on certain characteristics of reporting in the *Times* with respect to Germans and the German situation, and then review in more detail what the *Globe and Mail* had to say about these subjects. The *Globe and Mail* relied on foreign correspondents of the *Times* for many news items on Germany and Hitler's activities, making it doubly important that its attitudes be assessed at least briefly.

The *Times* came to be the most important British newspaper for information on Germany, and many thought that the paper spoke for the

British government. This was not the case, and in fact it has been argued that the *Times* was privy to more information on Germany than the British government. Despite its significance, the *Times* was not unlike other British newspapers in much of its underlying philosophy. A study of the British press revealed that a common experience shaped the views of journalists reporting to British newspapers. They had served in the First World War and therefore had experienced its horrors first-hand. An undercurrent ran through the commentary these journalists wrote—there must not, under any conditions, be another war. Generally speaking, they blamed the Treaty of Versailles for the ills that threatened Europe and for unpleasant developments in Germany as well. Hitler's foreign policy was not normally condoned by the British press, but journalists often avoided confronting signs of German aggressive positioning. While attention was given to the mass rallies and parades as well as reactions to them, for example, the papers tried to downplay the potential implications of such events. Spectacle and theatre, not evidence of interest in war and territorial expansion, set the tone of British newspaper reporting concerning the rallies.[1]

Even though the *Times* was appalled at the arbitrary violence of the Hitler regime, the paper, like others, promoted appeasement and shuddered at the effects of the Treaty of Versailles on the contemporary state of Europe. For example, on August 4, 1937, the following appeared in the paper, with the headline "Stability and Change":

As the vision recedes of that summer night, twenty-three years ago today, when Great Britain dedicated herself to the hazard of war in defence of a small country and of our national safety, the memory of all that was suffered as a consequence of the great resolve becomes more rather than less poignant. As we survey the world around us we are assailed by the bitterness of doubt whether anything good or useful was accomplished by the dreadful slaughter that ensued.[2]

One problem, the paper continued, is that we took on too much in trying to save the world for democracy. We thought people would joyfully embrace it. Another problem is that we failed to take into account how the peace treaties would affect the vanquished.

Letters to the editor of the *Times*, in spite of abhorrence for much of German policy, revealed a particularly strong conciliatory point of view concerning Germans. "Anglo-German Relations. Abandoning the 'Anti' Attitude" read one headline. The two countries cannot get along until they understand what they have in common and where they differ forever, a reader argued in his letter to the paper. Britain will never tolerate suppression and persecution for political and religious reasons, and not because of offences against the law, this person elaborated. Persecution on the basis of race, England views with "a deep and generous indignation," he added. But Britain can act as a mediator to make relations closer between France and Germany, and thereby help the cause for peace, the writer explained. He noted also that Germany and England shared common interests—love of family, for example.[3] The *Times*, however, came to believe in British rearmament, both as a method of restraining Germany and therefore maintaining peace and as a bulwark against actions threatening British interests.

While reports of the foreign correspondent for the *Times* living in Germany were commonly picked up by the *Globe and Mail* in Canada, the Canadian paper lacked the undertone of support for appeasement, interest in the effects of the Versailles Treaty, or concern with commonalities with Germans that dominated the *Times*. The Canadian paper was more focused on what appeared to be a developing irreversible path toward war than the more hopeful, appeasement-driven British paper. The *Globe and Mail* was, naturally, also more interested in American reactions to Hitler than the *Times*, whose attention remained centred on European attitudes. The failure of Americans to support the League of Nations, for example, seemed more important for world peace than the mistakes of the Versailles Treaty to the *Globe and Mail*. There was a distancing of the North American paper from European affairs in spite of firm loyalty to the British Empire. The *Globe and Mail* saw events as they unravelled in Europe from an outsider point of view. Canadians were onlookers rather than participators in the changing European situation. Both the *Times* and the *Globe and Mail*, however, concentrated on the reporting of events, political statements, the political implications of both, and general reaction to all of the above in countries outside Germany. Neither attempted in any serious way to learn what the average German thought about political developments in Germany or effects on the international scene.

The contents of the *Globe and Mail* for the period immediately preceding Wegenast's trip, that is 1936 until late February 1938, perhaps most significantly contributed to the shaping of Wegenast's thinking. The Toronto-based publication served as a national paper for Canada and reflected much of the general culture of the country. Some of Wegenast's biases clearly dovetailed with that culture: his strong attachment to Britain and British things, for example. "Empire Is World's Hope" was the headline of an article reporting on a speech given to the Empire Club in the fall of 1936. The speaker pointed out that the British Empire was unlike any earlier one and was the world's hope today. It is of vital interest that the British way of life be promoted in the world, he stated, adding that no one would deny that.

> Those who study current history must realize that strong among whatever motives may be actuating certain bellicose foreign Powers is an intense jealousy of the British Empire. Internal weakness, developing in that Empire, must have disastrous effects upon all its constituent parts and throw world progress back into the dark ages.... So long as the United States remains aloof from world affairs, Britain and the Empire are the sole remaining barriers against unscrupulous and barbarous aggression. Break down those barriers by whatever means, and the upstart "isms" of rival autocracies would plunge the world into a war in which the weak and unprotected nations must be crushed—however noble their ideals, however loudly they may insist on their "neutrality"—and the British ideals of freedom, justice and enlightenment must perish.[4]

The speaker added that Italy, Germany and Japan were threats to the British Empire.

A German author, Johannes Stoye, published a book in 1935 in Munich that praised the British. The book, named *The British Empire*, was translated into English in 1936 and found a ready audience in Canada.[5] From the diary and Wegenast's Sigfrid Schmidt file it is clear that this book (or at least discussion concerning it in the paper) deeply affected him and shaped some of his views about Germans. "Empire Inspires Respect," the *Globe and Mail* announced, and continued as follows.

> Discussing British characteristics, [the author, Stoye] declares that the Briton "upholds the ideal of the gentleman, the teachings of fair-play and self-control."... He concludes that the disintegration of the Empire is neither approaching, nor desired even by other Powers.... This tribute from a former foe, its favourable acceptance in Germany and other countries, and the foreign courtesy to the Empire already referred to, should be sufficient evidence that Britain remains as strongly as ever the guardian of world peace.[6]

A book review on Stoye's *British Empire* appeared shortly after in the paper.

> German Lauds British Empire in Analysis of Its Character.... One of the most popular books in Germany last year was Dr. Stoye's

long work on the British Empire, its origin, structure and future, particularly as to whether dissolution has set in. The appearance of the book this month in London began a wave of approval and popularity there, which is natural as the book is entirely flattering to English character and national prospects. What seems to have been overlooked is that "British Empire" comes from a besieged country seeking friends, and to whom the friendship or enmity of Great Britain spells success or failure. Though it emanates from an individual, he inhabits a country in which Government approval is essential to the publication of a book, let alone its open popularity. Coupled with these reflections, the last page confesses self-interest: "Weak states are an incentive to war, and peace-loving Germany has therefore an interest in inner consolidation and strengthening of the British Empire." Again, German naiveté has confirmed what otherwise could only have been inferred. This is not a disinterested work of scholarship: Germany is bidding for an ally.[7]

The author's research is biased, the book reviewer added, and based on the thoughts of ultra-Imperialists.

The paper dealt with the issue of anti-Semitism as an international as well as a German problem between 1936 and 1938. In Toronto it seemed to be provoked by the Palestine crisis that Britain was attempting to negotiate. The *Globe and Mail* reported in 1937,

The second move in the month to discriminate against Jews in Toronto sport was revealed Sunday, when St. Andrew's Golf Club acted to bar its course to all but Gentiles. [The largely Gentile players, members, and many others who were pay-as-you-play wanted this.] "We have to protect our business," [the secretary of the club told the paper]. "The great majority of our people are Gentiles, and we have to respect their wishes in this matter. It was not a very pleasant thing to have to do, but everyone has to protect their own interests, and that's what we are doing." The sign at the entrance of the club read: "After Sunday, June 20, this course will be restricted to Gentiles only. Please do not question this policy. (Signed) J.G. Reid, Secretary." The word "Gentiles" was in italics.

The paper noted that Jews who used the club were outraged, and stated that "a group of Jewish players at the club plan to organize to investigate the causes of the ban, and prepare for action against similar moves in the future."[8]

Within two weeks the paper reported in a headline, "Britain Endorses Jewish and Arab Separate States," that is, a plan to split Palestine into two states in order to end fifteen years of Jewish/Arab bloodshed. Until accomplished, the British recommended that Jews and Arabs stay in their own section, not cross to the other, and not sell land to any member of the other, the paper explained. "The British Government has accepted, in general, the conclusions of the Palestine Royal Commission, and thus once more has invoked John Bull's well-known faculty for settling conflicts by compromise. That the report was not expected to be received by Jews and Arabs with unanimous approval is shown by the precaution taken to curb demonstration."[9] Within days of this announcement, the *Globe and Mail* informed its readers in a large headline: "Lurid Sign Warns Jews off East End Beach" in Toronto. "When residents in the vicinity of Victoria Park Avenue in East Toronto went down to the beach ... yesterday morning they found a sign ... with letters three feet high," stretching 75 yards. "It read in full: 'Britain gave you Jerusalem: for God's sake leave us this beach.'"[10]

Reports on anti-Semitism in other countries outside Germany appeared in the press. In 1936 the *Globe and Mail* noted that Conrad Hoffman (who was director of the Department of Jewish Evangelization for the Presbyterian Church in the United States, and who also worked for a British committee trying to encourage Christians to get along with Jews) believed anti-Semitism was on the rise in England. The paper commented on Hoffman's experiences. He had received pamphlets on the street of the town of Gullford (perhaps should read Guildford) that denounced the opening of shops by Jews. "Is this England or Palestine?" the pamphlets asked, and stated "The Jews have arrived in town!" Libel had also been circulated in Parliament. Hoffman had visited countries in Europe over the question of anti-Semitism. A Polish statesman stated that one million Jews would be driven out of Poland annually. "Where would they go?" Hoffman questioned. Russia, the one non-Christian country, alone was offering domicile to the Jews.[11] By early 1938, the situation had become more violent. The *Globe and Mail* reported that fascists marched through Jewish sections of London, chanting slogans like "Perish Judah," "We gotta get rid of the Yids," and "Roll on the pogrom." Shops were wrecked and people assaulted: "Dirty Jew bastards ... get back to Palestine." The paper also reported that the slurs "hooked-nosed, yellow-skinned, dirty Jewish swine" and "venereal-ridden vagabonds" were used in a meeting of Fascists. Neither the attacks nor the words seemed to trigger arrests by the police.[12]

The problem in Germany received much more attention as anti-Semitic activity escalated after the passing of the Nuremberg Laws in 1935. "German

Jews Lose Status," the *Globe and Mail* stated in 1937, continuing: "The Jew has virtually disappeared from the main currents of German life. Official bans imposed by the Nazi regime have forced him into a cultural, social, political and economic ghetto. No part of the Nazi's twenty-five-point program has been realized more completely than that calling for elimination of Jews from Germany's public life." Signs saying "'no Jews allowed in public places' are not necessary," the paper pointed out, "because Jews don't go there. Jews are now outlawed from doing much of anything—all department stores that were formerly owned by Jews in Berlin—are no longer."[13] The *Globe and Mail* reported on the virulent and vicious attacks on Jews by Julius Streicher, who owned the strongly anti-Semitic paper, the *Stormer*: "Julius Streicher, fanatic Nazi editor and Germany's No. 1 Jew-baiter," and spoke of Helmuth Hirsch, the American Jew who was executed after going to Germany with a plan to kill Streicher. "'I was happy,' said Streicher, 'when I read in the newspapers that this Jew Hirsch came to Germany to assassinate me. The action of this Jew showed me that I was following the right path.... We will see to it that the Jews never succeed in coming out of retreat to defeat their enemy.'"[14]

In August 1937 there were reports of Hitler suppressing Rotary Clubs in Germany because of an assumed association of the organization with Jews. "Rotary Clubs Banned in Germany as Anti-Nazi," the Canadian paper's headline read, and reporting on the topic followed under such subheadings as: "Hide-Out for Jews—Chief Justice Orders All Members of Party to Resign; Hints Penalties—Membership Includes Many Prominent Men." The campaign against Rotary stemmed from the fact that it was not anti-Semitic, the paper explained, and added that the Nazis argued it was an American organization run by Jews. "Leadership in the Nazi State and membership in Rotary cannot go together," the Nazi party had announced, according to the *Globe and Mail*. The past president of Toronto Rotary was not surprised, the paper reported. "'I visited Germany this summer and I gathered that Rotary was suffering from restraints imposed by the Government. If the chief reason for the ban is because Rotary is not anti-Semitic, then we plead guilty to the charge. Rotary is definitely not anti-Semitic.... We want to create a better understanding between business men irrespective of religion,' he added."[15]

The *Globe and Mail* quoted statements released by Nazi authorities about laws against Jews in early 1938.

The Nazi economic press listed measures that should be taken against Jews. 1) Foundation of new Jewish participation in business enterprises should be forbidden. 2) Jews should be prevented from profiting by improvements in the economic situation. 3) German businesses should be strengthened in order to facilitate the passing of Jewish enterprises into German hands. 4] Jewish participation in the processing of transferring Jewish enterprises from Jewish to German hands should be eliminated.[16]

The *Globe and Mail* reported that German Canadians were finding things none too easy as a result of the rising hate in Germany, but seemed unsure about their pleas for consideration as a minority. "Tolerance of the Majority," read its headline, which reported on a convention that took place in Western Canada.

German-Canadians, in convention at Regina, according to a press dispatch, "demanded equality and respect, and not merely tolerance." They are entitled to both as law-abiding Canadian citizens who have come to this country to live as British citizens and uphold British ideas. Why should it be necessary to demand that which is conceded in a democratic Dominion? Perhaps if those of alien races who protest like this—and the Germans are not the only ones—examined themselves they might discover that what they believe to be lack of equality and respect for them is lack of approval for practices and ideals they promote. Canada must be regarded as a British-Canadian country in essence and principle. Probably Canadians as a whole expect representatives of the various races settling here to accept the circumstances and conditions they find. They cannot be expected to view with equanimity efforts to reorganize and transform a British country into something foreign. German-Canadians who prefer the Nazi saints and the Swastika to "God Save the King" and the Union Jack do not belong here, but in Germany. No one can deny the right and desirability of keeping alive memories of the homeland in song and folklore, but the laws, customs and languages of the adopted country must become those of the new people if we are to build a united nation.... Much is being said these days about the rights of the minority. It is time to speak of the rights of the majority.[17]

Three particularly significant international issues that related to Germany and Germans dominated the press between mid-1936 and early 1938: namely the situation around Hitler's involvement in the Spanish Civil War and the contingent threat of European war, persecution of the Christian Church by the Nazis, and developments in Austria.

A little background to the *Globe and Mail*'s reporting on the Spanish situation is necessary. After his successful and untroubled re-militarization of the Rhineland in March 1936, Hitler took a more aggressive stance toward foreign policy—and an interventionist one as well—which fuelled a rising fear, palpable in the paper. When the Spanish Civil War broke out in July 1936, Hitler took immediate action. German planes arrived in Spain almost immediately to help the right-wing rebels, led by Franco, who wanted to form a dictatorship and in the process oust the left-wing government. The German presence escalated quickly. In November of that year, German forces, under the name of the Condor Legion, landed at Cadiz and formally recognized Franco's regime as the government of Spain. The activity of Mussolini and of the Soviet Union (which provided aid to the left-wing faction) in the Spanish problem reinforced the sense that world war was becoming a real possibility. In fact the Spanish problem—and the issue contingently of war—particularly with respect to Germany's rising and aggressive intervention—took more space in the *Globe and Mail* than what was happening in Germany over most of 1936 and 1937. What were Hitler's plans for other countries? Talk of invasions of Austria and Czechoslovakia was in the air.

As Christmas neared in 1936, the *Globe and Mail* pondered the issue of world peace under the headline "London on Alert for Large Scale Military Thrust."

> A vague fear gripped European Capitals tonight that Germany might use the holiday season for some spectacular military or diplomatic coup. From Berlin came a report that a political decision of such importance impended that Adolf Hitler had abandoned all plans for a Christmas in the country, and would remain in Berlin. The London press openly speculated on the possibility that German troops might march either into Czechoslovakia or Spain. Germany's decree preventing men of military age from leaving the country without special permission intensified the rumors.[18]

On Christmas day, the paper asked, "What Next, Hitler? ... The 'sudden new anxiety' in the British press over a possible Hitler holiday coup does not sit well with Foreign Secretary Anthony Eden's 'no-cause-for-worry' speech in the House of Commons a few days ago." The growing muddle in international affairs makes the press worried, the paper added.[19]

The Führer at last spoke, only to increase fear of war throughout the world. "London Shocked by Its Vague, Negative Tone," the paper stated,

on the first day of February 1937. "Fear spread across Europe today that
Fuehrer Adolf Hitler, in his historic speech in the Reichstag Saturday, has
slammed the door on efforts of European statesmen to bring about a lasting
peace." Hitler refused to deal in any way with Russia, the paper stated and
continued as follows: "Hitler roared about the unfairness of the Versailles
treaty and formally removed Germany's signature of it. He demanded the
return of Germany's former colonies, railed against any agreement with
Russia, and refused to join other countries in economic trade agreements—
especially if any included Russia. He divided the world between communism
and fascism." Reeling from Hitler's speech, the paper continued the
next day to review what he had said under such titles as: "Germany to
Force Issue of Colonies"—"Nazi Demands Are Prepared; War Talk Gains."
General agreement outside Germany was that Hitler's speech did nothing
for the cause of peace, the paper noted, and added, "On the contrary, it is
generally admitted that the speech of the Nazi dictator will compel European
democracies to strive still harder to build up effective armaments. A study
of the two-hour oration by responsible observers discloses nothing to relieve
the steadily deepening gloom. Those who listened to the Fuehrer's speech
were impressed by the tones of deepest scorn in his references to the
League of Nations and the ferocity of his attack on Russia."[20]

Sensing rising tension outside Germany, the Nazi party pulled back on
threats. On February 13, the paper reported under the headline "No War
Danger Goebbels Says" that Goebbels told a mass meeting there would be no
war in Europe because Germany had successfully rearmed. "We will attack
no one," Goebbels said.[21]

The Nazi promise of non-aggression did not trigger enduring relief
outside Germany. Open and highly publicized scorn for Hitler and the Nazi
regime erupted in North America in March 1937. Anti-Semitism, combined
with the threat to world peace that resulted from intervention in Spain's
civil war, seemed to drive the acrimony. In retaliation, the Germans
ordered apologies, threatening further reprisals, the Canadian paper told
its readers. "Nazi Press in Fury at New York Mayor for Gibe at Hitler," the
Globe and Mail noted, after Fiorello La Guardia stated at a meeting of the
Women's Division of the American Jewish Congress that a "brown-shirted
fanatic" should be starring in a "chamber of horrors" at the 1939 World's
Fair. "Germany's Government-controlled press tonight angrily demanded
an official reprimand of [La Guardia] for supposedly insulting Adolf Hitler,
and hinted retaliation if La Guardia's suggestion that Der Fuehrer's statue
be placed in a 'chamber of horrors' were not sponged off the record." The
German press "intimated that Germany will take 'an interest in American

events which might not be precisely pleasant unless the Mayor's allegedly slanderous words are retracted.'"[22]

Comments made by the German press did not come from German officials, but the press printed only what the government approved—a fact fully understood by the Canadian paper. The *Globe and Mail* carried comments made in the German Press—"New York's Chief Jew, La Guardia, filthily insults Fuehrer." (La Guardia's mother was partially Jewish.) A Berlin paper stated, "This shameless Jew lout dares doubt the Fuehrer's love of peace.... This Jewish apostle of hate with his thieves' den mentality cannot conceive what it means to slander the Fuehrer of a nation of 70,000,000. At the same time one cannot avoid the conviction that the White House should be powerful enough to forbid this." When La Guardia was told of German indignation, he said they were right to complain, for "I know of no artist, or designer who can adequately fill, paint or carve anything that will adequately depict either the personalities of the Nazi Government, Hitler himself, or the type of government he is giving." The American government responded by apologizing but also saying it was a regrettable incident, and nothing could be done to stop this type of talk, the *Globe and Mail* explained.[23]

"La Guardia, Scorning U.S. Apology, Again Slaps Hitler," read a headline of the paper, which added that the American State Department had formally apologized to Hitler. La Guardia was undeterred after two rebukes from Washington, the paper noted, reporting that La Guardia said, "I stand by what I said, and I repeat it again. I referred to a brown-shirted fanatic who is menacing the peace of Europe. Mr. Hitler and his Government were quick to recognize that I meant him. I don't know whether it is a guilty conscience or my power of description, in either case it is irrelevant." The German press couldn't understand, the paper added, why Roosevelt didn't control La Guardia better.[24] The *Globe and Mail* reported that the American ambassador to Germany had protested against the filthy language in the German press that surfaced over the La Guardia affair, and added that the ambassador had told the German government that articles were "'unparalleled in course and indecent character and shocking to all decent minds.' The protest was made as a result of publication in Government-controlled newspapers of attacks on American officials, 'civilization,' and 'womanhood,' growing out of the suggestion of [La Guardia] ... that Chancellor Adolf Hitler's statue be placed in a 'chamber of horrors.'" The ambassador reported to the Germans that "the American people saw no justification in such 'sweeping vituperation, unfounded statements and attacks on American womanhood and institution.'" The ambassador pointed out that freedom of speech was part of American life.[25]

The *Globe and Mail* reported on a huge meeting that took place in New York, during which Hitler was slammed again and again as a monster who was threatening world peace. Hitler was booed and shouted at, La Guardia hailed. One speaker said "this brutality breaking through the sentiments of centuries of civilization—there must be some explanation for it, and I think there is. But that explanation will be found in the psychopathic wards of hospitals and not in historical analysis. This rule by force—this political animalism—there is something sadistic, perverted, abnormal, unclean about these welterers in human blood, these sybarites in cruelty, these voluptuaries in the misery of mankind." "They don't even understand the meaning of free speech and the fact that La Guardia had every right to say what he did," stated the paper.[26] The Germans responded again to this attack by La Guardia and others at the big rally.[27]

At the end of March and in April 1937 German planes and a small of number of Italian planes bombed two Spanish towns that opposed Franco, killing thousands of civilians and in the process escalating the threat of world war. In May, when the Spanish bombed the German warship *Deutschland*, the Germans retaliated by sending five warships to destroy the town of Almeria, "exacting a toll of about 100 lives in payment for the *Deutschland*'s twenty-four dead," the *Globe and Mail* stated, and continued:

> Never since the frightening times of 1914 has Europe faced a crisis so grave so crammed with warlike acts, threats and alignments. People gathered in the streets of London, Berlin, Rome, Paris and other European Capitals to discuss the swift and startling events that have loomed larger and larger day by day since the outbreak of the Spanish civil war last July 17th. They snatched up newspapers and sat around radio stations that rasped out the news in a dozen languages.[28]

The *Globe and Mail* told its readers that on May 31 Hitler had been "Told to Go Easy Lest He Plunge Europe into War," and expanded as follows: "France and Great Britain tonight warned Chancellor Adolf Hitler of Germany that, unless he abandons his acts of reprisal he may plunge Europe into a terrible war.... Germany and Italy tonight renounced their Spanish neutrality pledges and withdrew their support from the international non-intervention project.... Germany withdrew from the International Neutrality Committee, on which twenty-seven nations had struggled to prevent the Spanish holocaust from bursting its boundaries and becoming another world war."[29]

The ricocheting continued, as Hitler attempted to calm fears. "Reich Won't Start War, Says Hitler, But Ready to Strike if Attacked," a headline in the Canadian paper read on June 7. "Hitler tonight [June 6] told a mass meeting of 150,000 Bavarian Nazis that, despite recent events in Spain, Germany has no intention of starting a war, 'either today, tomorrow, or the day after tomorrow.'" This was his first speech, the paper added, "on the grave complications in Spain that brought all Europe to the brink of open war a week ago. He shouted a bold defence of the destruction of the Spanish loyalist seaport of Almeria by German warships—Germany's vengeance for the bombing of the 'pocket battleship' *Deutschland*." "'Germany will not suffer to be insulted or attacked,' the paper quoted Hitler as saying. 'If someone thinks he may throw bombs at our ships, then we shall show him that we do not stand for such things.... There is only one effective means against the Jewish-Bolshevist clique—to hit back when they attack.'"[30] It appeared that Germany would start to cooperate with the neutrality efforts of other nations, the *Globe and Mail* reported hopefully. The paper was forced to admit a few days later, though, that despite calm in the Spanish crisis, no one knew what the future would bring. There was no evidence of a lasting solution.[31]

Although the Catholic Church was persecuted as well, it was the Nazi crusade against a Protestant Christian church that touched a particular nerve in Canadian, American, and British society. The complicated story of this church–Nazi struggle needs a short introduction in order to clarify the newspaper reporting that so incensed people, including Wegenast, as he shows in his diary.

The German Evangelical Church, which had united the Lutheran and Calvinist faiths in the country in the nineteenth century, appealed to the Nazis as a logical national church, and the party moved quickly to both dominate it and control it. Serious moves to Nazify it arose in 1933. Attempts to remove converted and Christianized Jews from the Evangelical Church by the Nazis turned a number of pastors against governmental control. These pastors saw allegiance to Christ and the teachings of the bible as more important than racial origin. A number of them joined together in 1934 to form a splinter church, the Confessing Church, which rejected the "Aryanization" of the Reich Church, or the German Evangelical Church. The Nazis tried to suppress the Confessing Church and began arresting pastors who supported it. Central to the Confessional movement was Martin Niemoeller, pastor of Dahlem, a suburb of Berlin. He was arrested in July 1937. His brother suffered the same fate shortly after. For foreigners, the two Niemoellers personified a healthy and justified German resistance to Nazi power, and the headlines reporting their arrest were celebratory: "Leaders of Church Defy Nazis; Rev. Wilhelm Niemoeller Latest Placed under Arrest; Clerics Are Uniting; Protestants and Catholics Battle Common Enemy."

"Confessional Church leaders defied the Nazi religious policy today after the arrest of Rev. Wilhelm Niemoeller, pastor of St. Anne's Church in the suburb of Dahlem," the paper stated, and expanded as follows "Niemoeller, brother of Rev. Martin Niemoeller, arrested three weeks ago, was seized by secret police after a bold sermon in which he praised his brother's stand against Nazification of the Protestant Churches and an appeal that congregations stand fast against the threat of totalitarian ideology to religious freedom." The Confessional church leaders sent a manifesto out to all Evangelical pastors, the *Globe and Mail* explained, saying that "Niemoeller never has done anything but spread God's Gospel." He did not disquiet the people; the Nazis have by trying to take over control of the church.[32]

The Nazis were divided about the advisability of holding a trial for Martin Niemoeller. "Nazi Effort Being Made to Drop Trial," a *Globe and Mail* headline noted in August 1937, adding that "Berlin reports that party has split over Niemoeller case.... Indications tonight were that some Nazi quarters desired to drop trial proceedings against Rev. Martin Niemoeller, Protestant leader in the fight against Government regulation of church affairs." His trial had been postponed with no new date set, the paper added, and some ministers had been released.[33] No one knew what happened to Martin Niemoeller between then and early February 1938 when a trial was set, shortly before Wegenast left for Europe.

"Niemoeller Is Refused Public Trial," the *Globe and Mail* reported, and enlarged on the story. The pastor was brought to trial at a secret court, but he demanded a public hearing to show that he had done nothing against his country. Despite being imprisoned for seven months at Mosbit prison, he remained feisty. The judges, wearing swastikas, quickly dismissed this request for a public trial. "Immediately afterward the Gestapo (secret police) of Heinrich Himmler ordered the 'quarantine' of Niemoeller's colleagues." (Many Germans still admired Niemoeller for his work during the First World War.)[34] "Niemoeller, defiant, fires three lawyers, directs own defence," the paper continued. "Smarting under refusal of Nazi court to grant open trial, he spurns offer of new counsel." Niemoeller asked the judges why the press was allowed to call him a traitor when all he had done was to oppose Nazification of the German churches. Niemoeller fired his lawyers because they refused to ask for an open trial—saying it wouldn't work and would anger the judges, the paper explained and added, "the fact that the Government is aware of the pastor's wide popularity, particularly among the junkers and old-school army officers, was revealed ... when the prosecution announced that two or three of the five charges against him had been dropped."[35] But "the trial of Rev. Martin Niemoeller, leader of Protestant opposition to Nazi religious doctrine, on charges of treasonable activity, [continued on]," the *Globe and Mail* pointed out, "and the prosecution reversed a ruling favorable to the Lutheran pastor."[36] The trial, in fact, was a fiasco and he was released on March 2. As he left the prison gates, the Gestapo seized Niemoeller on Hitler's direct orders. Niemoeller was re-imprisoned in Sachsenhausen concentration camp. His re-incarceration aroused widespread opposition within and outside Germany, which proved to be an embarrassment for Hitler.[37] Niemoeller was imprisoned later at Dachau, but survived the war.

In the weeks before Wegenast left for his trip, the *Globe and Mail* concentrated on escalating events taking place in Austria. An authoritarian regime had been in place since 1933 when parliament had been permanently dissolved. In 1936 the Austrian chancellor and dictator, Kurt von Schuschnigg, had agreed to the principle that Austria was a German state and had allowed the Austrian Nazi party to hold positions in the government. Schuschnigg believed that these actions settled difficulties with Germany. Hitler saw the situation as a means of buying time before the eventual complete Nazi domination of Austria. By 1938 Schuschnigg's government had grown progressively weaker. Poverty still reigned in Austria and anti-Semitism was on the rise in the country. Coincidentally, a heightened sense of urgency seemed to grip Hitler with regard to the future of Austria. For one thing, it was hard to hide the level of rearmament in Germany from the rest of Europe. At the same time, other countries were rearming as well. The advantages Germany had within Europe might not last long.

In mid-February 1938 Hitler called a meeting with Schuschnigg and browbeat him into formal submission to German demands to co-ordinate Austrian-German foreign policy, collaborate in military expansion, and revoke any measures in place against the German or Austrian Nazi party.[38] From that time until mid-March, events moved swiftly, and ultimately led to the removal of Schuschnigg from power and the control of Germany over Austria.

"Adolf Hitler Achieves Domination of Austria," the paper announced February 16, 1938, shortly before Wegenast left Canada. When Hitler forced Kurt von Schuschnigg, Chancellor of Austria, by threat of military force, to put five Austrian Nazi sympathizers in his cabinet, the reports read, "Berlin Ultimatum Puts Five Nazis in Vienna Cabinet" and "Schuschnigg, long a bitter foe of Nazi penetration into Austria ... announced his capitulation"; "Nazis now hold control of the Austrian police. London and Paris expected to represent to Berlin how important it is to them that Austria maintains its independence"; "It appears that Germany and Austria were on the road to 'Gleichschaltung'[39]—harmonization—in domestic and international fields." "Although developments ... did not actually constitute 'Anschluss'[40]— Austrian–German union—they brought such a possibility sensationally nearer, a prominent observer commented."

The next day the paper carried the headline "Nazi Coup in Austria Hits Snag," and continued:

> Hitler's "Nazification" of the Austrian cabinet was understood to
> have met sudden defiance tonight when he sought to extend his
> "coup" to include control·of Austria's armed forces. Police meanwhile
> took stern measures to prevent disorders as prison gates were
> ordered thrown open for thousands of Nazi "martyrs" whose release
> was demanded by Germany.... Great Britain and France, fearful that
> Nazi penetration in Austria may be the groundwork of a German
> invasion eastward, agreed tonight to lodge representatives in Berlin
> and Vienna asking assurance that ... Hitler intends to preserve
> Austrian independence.[41]

Czechoslovakia was left as a democracy island in the middle of a Fascist sea. The British and French representatives in Berlin and Vienna "will ask in firm but polite terms, that immediate assurances of Austrian sovereignty be given," the paper stated and noted that the Czechs were reinforcing their borders with Austria. "Come the Dread Anchluss"—had been part of German thinking for a hundred years before Hitler.[42] The *Globe and Mail* quoted the views of an Australian on Hitler, who stated that Hitler's "chief delusion is that he is a deliverer, born to save all mankind, his chief strength in the German national tendency to play follow-the-leader," adding that Hitler's lack of education made him incapable of seeing more than one side of an issue. "And the same mental incapacity enables him to preserve intact his sense of the overruling Wagnerian rightness of every Nazi act."[43]

"Hitler Hastens to Nazify Austria," the headline stated on February 18, and bombarded readers with the following information: "German Arm Is Reaching into All Phases of Government"; "Danube Capital Gloomy but Reconciled to Inevitable"; "Czech–Nazi Foes Clash at Border." The paper expanded on the topics. Sudeten Czech Nazis clashed with opponents of the Nazi party, it said. Meetings took place in London over the situation in Austria, and the problem was discussed in both houses of parliament. Confusion prevailed over what the European situation meant.[44]

"Prime Minister Chamberlain stated that Britain should do everything in her power to maintain peace, and at the same time build herself to be so strong that no nation could attack her," the paper continued on February 19. Articles in the *Globe and Mail* that day enlarged on the story in the following fashion: "Nazis, who last night triumphantly looked forward to complete nazification of Austria, had to curb their optimism somewhat tonight when secrecy was lifted from some concessions ... Hitler had made. The concessions were in the realms of religion, 'Weltanschauung'[45]—world outlook—and acquiescence to Austrian Chancellor ... Schuschnigg's refusal to allow a plebiscite in Austria at this time."[46] "Hitler, it was announced, has arranged to take measures to uphold Austria's sovereignty by prohibiting the German Nazis from interfering in the conduct of Austrian internal affairs.... Meanwhile, Austria's first anti-Semitic decree, ordered by the new Nazi Minister of the Interior, was issued."[47]

Town mayors were ordered to cease cooperating with priests in baptizing Jews if the citizenship of the Jews was questioned. This affected the thousands of German Jews who fled Germany and went to Austria after the Nazi accession to power in Germany.[48]

On February 21 the paper reported on the long-awaited, three-hour speech Hitler gave in the Reichstag on foreign policy: "Hitler Heralds Wider German Rule; Tells World Britain Must Yield Colonies.... In dramatic speech, Der Fuehrer declares Reich will defend freedom of Germans in Austria and Czechoslovakia, and warns army is prepared to meet any challenge." In his speech, Hitler asserted that the British press were imperilling peace. The speech "lacked any pledge to uphold Austrian independence and integrity as had been anticipated in many capitals.... Hitler made it clear that Germany will ignore Great Britain and France, as well as other Western powers, in carrying out the new phase of her international policy to 'defend the political freedom of race-conscious Germans living beyond the frontiers of the Reich.'" The Führer stated that Germany would never restore friendship with Britain until Germany's war-lost colonies were restored.[49] Meanwhile the problems in Austria were mounting. "Thousands of Austrian Nazis, many of them just out of prison, swarmed through the streets tonight behind Swastika flags shouting 'Heil Hitler' as police mobilized to prevent clashes" with [Chancellor of Austria] Schuschnigg's storm troopers.[50] Schuschnigg met with Jews, saying they had nothing to fear in Austria, that Hitler's "Drang Nach Osten"[51]—road to the east—lay in Czechoslovakia. Hitler had no interest in any international conferences, the paper reported, going on to say that the Germany people stood behind Hitler and National Socialism.[52] It quoted

Hitler as saying, "I assure the world of the deep and sincere love of peace on the part of the German people, and also that their love of peace has nothing to do with a weak renunciation of cowardice and those who believe they can attack us with impunity will find iron resistance and see the German people united."[53]

The problems in Austria had become fused with bitter anti-Semitism. "Nazi Parade Routed by Vienna Police"—day-long riots in the city, the paper told its readers on February 22. Nazis were celebrating their penetration of the cabinet and the freeing of prisoners, which triggered an exodus of Jews from the country.

> Numerous wealthy Jews began leaving the country, seeking asylum until the demonstrations died down. Many began leaving ..., fearing that Adolf Hitler's address would touch off anti-Jewish campaigns in Austria. Various Jewish real estate owners hastily tried to sell out their properties. The Nazis, "freed" by Hitler, massed at noon before the university to demonstrate their strength. Students occupied the university buildings, shouting "Judah jump the twig!" (Go hang yourself), and "when Jewish blood drips from our knives everything will be well." Many girls were in the crowd. Catholic students and other anti-Nazis charged into them, and the fight began.[54]

The paper noted that anti-Semitic acts were happening in the United States at the same time: "Police at loss when [an American] Jewish dentist [was] slain.... War hero, driven out by Nazis, murdered in Chicago." He had left Germany a year ago, because he was a Jew (his wife was not), and he was a German war hero with six medals for bravery. No one knew why he was killed.[55]

Over the last few days before Wegenast left home, the *Globe and Mail* reported on the continuing deterioration of the situation in Europe and the acceleration of race hatred: One headline read: "Fear of Nazis Grips Austria, Jews Suicide." The following article stressed the gloomy atmosphere in Vienna, especially among Jews. "Vienna's customary gaiety was absent as Austria found herself increasingly under the influence of a Germany which hopes to extend her power throughout central Europe," the paper explained.[56] "Czechs are prepared to ward off attacks alone.... Czechoslovakia is ready to defend herself against sudden attack without waiting for outside help." The Czechs were waiting to hear what Schuschnigg had to say—hoping that he would stand for independence of Austria—and also what Britain had to say, wanting a clear idea of what that country's foreign policy was, the paper stated. "As riots spread to the provinces of Austria and only one sixth of the working population pledged support of Schuschnigg's stand for independence, the headline read, "Nazis Spread Grim Terror over Austria." A British shift toward the dictator "cleared the way for German expansion in Central Europe."[57]

"Schuschnigg's Defiance Inflames Nazis," a headline in the paper read on one of the last days that Wegenast was still in Ontario. Berlin was angered when Schuschnigg announced that "Nazi elements will remain outlawed.... Schuschnigg's assertion that Austria will 'fight to the death' to maintain her full independence were described here [Berlin] as being ineffectual in so far as preventing any 'development of Nazification' in Austrian internal affairs." Schuschnigg claimed that Hitler had pledged to maintain Austria's independence, the paper reported. "The Nazis contended, however, that their inroads in Austria will continue regardless of what Schuschnigg said or how he said it.... Declaration that Hitler is sworn to uphold Austrian independence provokes wild riots [in Vienna]." Nazis raged through the city at Schuschnigg's words and counter-demonstrations attacked them. Meanwhile Hitler announced that "Germany is about to take stern measures against 'Jewish provocateurs' stirring up hatreds." He lashed out at the foreign press as "poisoners": "We shall soon proceed energetically against the Jewish provocateurs in Germany. We know they are representatives of an international group and we shall deal with them accordingly. They can do nothing but lie, slander and incite hatred. We know they would not fight in any war, but would only profit by war."[58]

Up until the time that Wegenast left for his trip in the spring of 1938, the Canadian press's information on Germany and Germans tended to be in the nature of news reporting on events and speeches. Comments made by visitors to Germany, who were not correspondents of other newspapers, were relatively rare in the *Globe and Mail*.[59] One notable exception was commentary by Colonel George A. Drew, leader of the Ontario Conservatives after 1938.[60] In August 1937 he wrote to the *Globe and Mail* about what he had seen in Germany. Under the headline, "Finds Germany Touches Peak of Efficiency," the paper reported that Drew declared:

> It is nonsense to suggest that the German people appear oppressed, fearful and terrorized. Quite the contrary. No people in the world today look so uniformly fit and contented with their lot.... I believe that, so far as the internal situation is concerned, it is a race against time. The youth of Germany are, I am convinced, behind Hitler and what he is doing. Propaganda is having its effect and the Church is losing its hold over the youth amongst both Protestants and Catholics. It will be many years, perhaps, before the youth which

has been brought up to place Nazism before the old faiths will be the commanding majority.... Hitler is always the central figure. Hitler epitomizes Nazism in Germany and outside.[61]

It is worth further quoting Drew on the subject of Germany and military affairs. Nothing could more strongly reveal how dichotomous attitudes to German rearmament could be in Britain or her Commonwealth.

In considering the international picture and the possibilities of the future, the German army and air force have become the predominating factor. Those who talk loosely of forcing Germany's hand and imposing on them internal policies more favourable to our own point of view should spend a few weeks in Germany. There is no use talking to them about breaches of covenants, or the history which led up to the present situation. The simple and inescapable fact remains that the German army and air force are today the strongest in the world, and they are efficient with an efficiency which only comes from pride in the job they are doing.

Almost without exception, the people of Germany want the friendship of the British Empire. This is particularly so among members of the army and air force. Every Canadian ... who has visited Germany has found nothing but cordiality among German veterans.

I am not forgetting for a moment all that Canada suffered and that the rest of the world suffered as a result of German militarism in the past, but I am firmly convinced that there is in Germany today a spirit of friendliness and an actual desire for the assurance of peace than can be turned into useful channels, and produce international understandings, which in themselves will be the best way to end the abuses of the Nazi regime.[62]

A few days later the paper augmented Drew's remarks printed earlier, but in a rather ambiguous way. Headlines for his article contained comments made by Drew and read as follows: "Capable of Governing: Like Entering New World to Return from Continent; Buoyant, United: Leads in Recovery and Solution of Social Problems." Drew expanded as follows:

It is like stepping into a new world to return to Great Britain from Europe. In the dictatorships one is constantly reminded that freedom of speech and freedom of expression have disappeared. Private correspondence is rigidly censored and statements unsatisfactory to the Government lead to a request for immediate departure or possibly worse.... Great Britain has ridden the storm serenely. Great Britain has found a way to meet the threat of fascism or any other form of dictatorship.[63]

The editor of the *Globe and Mail* added to this commentary by saying, "Colonel Drew has applied keen logic to a practical situation. It required fortitude to ferret out the disillusioning truth, to depart from the prepared route in a country where everyone is under suspicion and state the facts. His British idealism, rare courage and brilliant intellect have all been well employed in disclosing European realities and especially Communist dictatorship and sham."[64]

These comments by and about Drew echo what he had said in a delivery to the Empire Club in October 1935, after an extended trip to Europe the summer before, and the comments written about his talk at the time. It is apparent from the Empire Club speech (but not from the paper's 1937 reporting) that Drew talked to Germans—sometimes official Nazi Party members, sometimes important businessmen—but it is also clear that he did so in English.[65] It does not appear that Drew went out among the people, where speaking German would have been a necessity. His feel for what constituted general thought was, therefore, restricted. As a public and political figure, Drew continued to discuss the European situation in various places in Ontario. By the fall of 1937 he argued that war seemed unlikely; Hitler had become polite. But more important, it seemed to Drew, Britain had decided to rearm.[66]

In January 1938, the American ambassador to Germany, William E. Dodd, resigned his Berlin post "in bitter opposition to Hitler's national-socialism," and stated that in four years Hitler had killed more political opponents than Charles II of England over twenty years.[67] "Mankind is in grave danger, but Democratic Governments seem not to know what to do," the *Globe and Mail* quoted him: "If they do nothing, Western civilization, religious, personal and economic freedom is in grave danger. Another world war would almost certainly wreck the Governments and people of our time." The paper went on to blame the United States as much as any other country for this state of affairs, because the American people would not support the League.[68] Within days an official German protest against Dodd's anti-Hitler speech was presented to the American Secretary of State, the paper stated. The secretary responded by saying that in the United States the constitution guaranteed freedom of speech, and that since Dodd had resigned his position with the government, as a private citizen he had the right to say what he liked and was no longer an agent of the views of the government.[69]

When Wegenast left for Europe, he had read a great deal about German aggression, anti-Semitism, attacks on the German Christian Church, and the Austrian situation. Regardless of the accuracy of the reporting, no *Globe and Mail* reader could fail to sense the rising crescendo of fear and concurrent threat of war inherent in the words the paper printed. The paper, however, provided no really comprehensive commentary on general German reactions to the apparent escalating danger. First-hand observations of people who went to Germany were rare in the paper—Drew and Dodd being notable exceptions. Drew's words implied German acceptance of Hitler's activities; at the same time he saw little threat to enduring peace. Dodd, on the other hand, while making no mention of German sentiment, emphasized the danger to Western civilization that lay behind Hitlerism. The paper offered little discussion about the validity of these conflicting points of view, or on how German thinking might influence the course of events.

Convinced of the dangers Germany posed to world peace and probably aware of diverse opinion on the subject as well, Wegenast intended to learn what Germans thought of Hitlerism, in order to better understand just how dangerous the situation was. How likely was it that there would be a war? Was the *Globe and Mail* justified in provoking fear in its readers? How influential was German opinion in preventing war? Were Canadians really aware of the true nature of Hitlerism? These were questions that Wegenast hoped to find answers to.

THE DIARY

3

Hamilton, Ontario. February 24, 1938

Well, I am away. After several tentative starts I have now got as far as the Wentworth Arms. But even this much is worthwhile. The moment I was actually off ... I began to feel a certain sense of lightness—of relief—a funny sort of curly springiness in my insides—a negation of fatigue. Dr. Oille is right: These are my words but in effect what he said: It is fatigue, whatever that is, (that was his expression) that is the cause of hypertension. The therapeutic value of the Nauheim treatments and others like them consists in building up a practice—and attitude—of non-fatigue; calling into play for this purpose the faculties physical, mental, and whatever else there are. Hence the practice of prescribing changes of air, of scene, etc. Hence also the necessity of "kidding," if possible, the patient— the importance of suggestion, for which, Dr. Oille has the temerity to say, I am a good subject.

February 25, 1938

But this begins hypochondriacally. But it did feel good to be off—no end of good. Even if I did not get any further than the Wentworth Arms. The Court House opposite looked different. I could thumb my nose at it.... And so the leisurely start in the morning—no appointments, no definite allotment of distance for the day. Yes, I am away, and what a swell idea this car is. Home is where the car is.

On board the Exeter. March 1, 1938

I sail the ocean blue once more. The first half-hour while the rest of the passengers were observing the wonders of the Empire State Building I was writing letters of acknowledgement to be dropped off by the pilot. When that was done I found Ellis Island far on the port horizon.... It seems altogether like a crowd in the best hotel in a U.S. town of about 4200. Oh, there is the odd individual who might have been a candidate for Congress. And there seem to be some representatives of decayed European aristocracy ...

The first meal—supper—hardly dinner. They seemed to aim to have it at six but it didn't quite come off—confusion, disorganization. About an hour before a fellow came through the corridors sounding a sort of xylophone and announcing that reservations for tables were being made in the dining room. I went down. Three or four persons were crowding into a corner at the left of the door of the dining room and craning their necks to read the names on a series of tickets, stuck on toothpicks on a little table. The little chief steward seemed to be in charge but objected to being crowded. He pleaded for time to make up his mind about the disposition of the toothpicks; so I left. When I got along about 6:45 after "Last call for supper" was announced (as in a dining car) the steward was still uncertain where to put me. I told him my preference was for, say, a family that spoke French. He n'en savait rien but suggested a certain table where there were some "nice people." I asked him if they were from the U.S. to which he replied with some enthusiasm in the affirmative. I resumed the quest for French people. Finally in desperation he set me down at a side table for two, remarking we could "see about [more permanent placement] later."

It was slow work. I drank my glass of water and the one opposite and ate most of the celery and olives before anything happened. When I had slowly progressed through the soup to red snapper another fellow turned up to puzzle the steward. I don't think he had stipulated anything but the steward did not know what to do with him, so he set him down opposite me to eat and "see." I went on reading "Armance" for the next twenty minutes while nothing was happening to him. Then I commiseratingly observed, "you are not having much luck." He immediately got into verbal (oral) action with "Christ, this is awful" etc., etc. He was wild-eyed at the humiliation. I was making slow progress myself and he was not starting. He had adequate things to say about the incompetence of the waiter—never mind the rest—but this guy was <u>tough</u>. They couldn't just do that to him. Just for that he would have his meals in his cabin. The waiter was in truth pretty hard to bear.... When I explained to him that I had drunk ... my tablemate's glass of water he coolly took my empty glass and filled it for my friend. I went some distance in emulating my friend's profanity in my comments to the waiter, who, on his part, admitted that his action had been a "mistake."

So a good time was had. .... And there is a young woman sitting alone at the bar, talkative with the bar-keeper—now she is drinking what looks like a Tom Collins. Her hair is a well-tended red.

Next day. March 2, 1938

The xylophone rang for lunch at 11:30. The second call at 11:45. I don't suppose they ever heard of afternoon tea except as having something to do with the Battle of Lexington. But let me not be unfair. Wait till five o'clock this afternoon before making up our minds. Most of those at the table at noon took steak and kidney pie. The red-haired beauty is at a table near ours. Now she is picking her teeth. And they are going to have boat drill this afternoon. They would. They have it at least seven times a trip, so someone said. I have never seen one on any other ship.

Yes, they did have tea, so they told me. It was all over when I asked for it. That was after the boat drill, which took place at 4:30. Yes, they had that and I joined in—put my life preserver on and went to Station Number Six. Glad I did, for it was in charge of the Purser, who seems a decent guy. It might have hurt him if I hadn't turned up.

Evening, March 2, 1938

It is likely that the average American has as high a percentage of butter-fat in the milk of his human kindness as any other breed (not a "nice" simile, but let it go). Why be so superior to them?— especially when the superiority doesn't make them mad.

It is just possible, dear reader, that you may detect in the following pages—or you may possibly have already noticed—a certain indisposition on the part of the writer toward things United Statesan. As a resident of the largest country in America I do not concede to the people of the United States the right to be referred to as "American" except as including Canadians, Mexicans etc. But you may possibly observe, let us say, something approaching lack of enthusiasm for people and things which might be regarded as something like one hundred per cent United Statesan? Well, take a look at the underlined parts of the following pages from the folder advertising the very cruises we are taking. And in order to avoid any misapprehension let me say at once that this literature (and art)

would have been conclusive against my taking this cruise, had it not
been that in every other respect than those held out in the literature
[it suited my purpose]. "On 'Yankee Cruise' ships you avoid that
heterogeneous mingling with uncongenial minds—no need to stamp
yourself as being different, or wonder what the crew is mumbling
about, or whether someone is pretending to misunderstand you, nor
need you miss the best and quickest of jokes ... home topics and
things of common American interest are proper subjects."

On board, Gibraltar. March 11, 1938

Last night culminated for me in a social victory. It was the
occasion of the fancy dress costume party—the first in which I had
participated in twenty years. The women tempted me—Mrs. Holmes
and Mrs. Leffman. And they enlisted others to my undoing.
Mrs. Leffman proposed the character which, after some elaboration,
turned out to be a Conception of the Shipwrecked Old Lady who
didn't believe in Boat Drill.

The costume included my white silk pajamas, a pink silk
nightgown (Mrs. Douglas's) a vermillion wrapper (Mrs. Douglas's), one
lady's silk stocking (hanging down) one patent leather shoe, one bare
foot in red slipper, one life preserver, with legs put through where the
arms are intended, a head of cork-screw curls (of untwisted rope) the
cap of a stewardess, a red bandana handkerchief, a blue hot-water
bottle, an alarm clock, rouge, lip-stick—all put on me con amore, to
the great delight of my lady neighbours of the semi-private verandah
and those adjoining. Result: fame, social prestige and First Prize.

Tonight. Captain's table. Presentation of prizes. Then Bingo.
To-morrow a.m. early Marseilles.

**By the middle of March, while still on board the ship, Wegenast had begun to
see how important but demanding his journal was. He interjected comments
under no dates, such as the following.**

My dear Journal, Chronicle, Memoir or Odyssey, or whatever we are
going to call you, you are getting to be a bit of a nuisance. You fill
up every bit of time which I might otherwise have for relaxation. But
I know I shall be sorry afterwards if I don't get things down before
they fade away.

There is this about you, Journal; you sharpen my dulled powers
of observation and memory. And I find myself conning (not a bad

*word) over phrases and words for you. I suppose that is the way
writers get; and what enables them afterwards to sit and write to the
accompaniment of the midnight oil.*

He started to philosophize on himself as well.

*I don't feel like recognizing any essential difference between myself
and any other set of human beings. Just because I happen to have
been born in, or have drifted into, a certain place, under certain
conditions of race, parentage, language, nationality, religion, social
and economic status etc., etc. is no reason why I should nest myself
there and stay there. It is not a matter of arrogance. Who am I that I
should be spared the sensations of a beggar, or a labouring man, etc?
On the other hand, who is anyone else that he should get away with
looking down on me? (If it makes any difference which way he looks.)*

**After spending a few days in Palestine, Wegenast thought about what he
had seen, particularly in Tel-Aviv. The new presence of Jews, many of them
American, was clearly changing the country.**

On board. March 23, 1938
*The business had a solid basis in dealings with the local agricultural
population. The expansion of this naturally brought about the
expansion of Tel-Aviv. For example, the growth of the trade in citrus
fruit meant a definite increase in business for Tel-Aviv. The growth in
trade brought with it a certain amount of dislocation and jealousy.
The native Arab population were not people who could be calmly
reasoned with. They would without proper forethought adopt some
course of action which reacted to make things worse for them rather
than better. For example, over some grievance they had banded
together in refusing to supply the people of Tel-Aviv with vegetables.
The result was that Jewish farmers who had been growing other
stuff went into vegetables and now they are underselling the Arabs
with very much better vegetables. The Arabs had lost the business.
Naturally they are sore. And just as naturally, they blame anything
else but themselves. That is human nature. It is the same way about
land. An Arab wants to sell his land. A Jew will give more than anyone
else. He takes the Jew's offer. The rest of the Arabs complain that
the Jews are crowding the Arabs out.... It is quite obvious that
the Jews in Palestine are out to make a showing of what they can
do. They are idealistic enough to overcome what one suspects to*

*be their indifference to sustained agricultural effort. We may be
wrong about that anyway. Various experiments seem to have shown
that there is nothing necessarily incompatible between a Jew and
ordinary farming.*

**After stopping at various ports throughout the Mediterranean, he disembarked
at Naples. He visited a number of Italian towns and cities, including Rome,
and then went on to Trieste, looking for Wegenast relatives. He wrote about
the visit when he had reached Venice.**

Venice. Evening of April 2, 1938

*Now I must write out my notes about my trip to Trieste this
afternoon. I hadn't really made up my mind until the last minute to
drive over. I was in something of a hurry to get into Austria ... but it
seemed to be too bad to be so near and not look up these relatives;
so in the morning I started for Trieste.... The approach to Trieste
is quite impressive. The road along the shore of the Gulf has been
terraced out of the mountain side. It is something like going along
the Hudson to New York, only the shore runs in a wide curve, with
Trieste visible through the haze of the spring afternoon. It is a real
"Corniche" with sub-tropical character in the making. For it turns out
that this approach is all new construction since the War and since
Italian occupation.*

*Arrived at Piazza Umberto #2. While I am getting something out of
the car a tall, pleasant Teutonic woman appears and asks if I am not
Herr Wegenast. She has seen the car from upstairs and has come
down to direct me. She is Frau Otto Wegenast. She is concerned
because I have said I am a bit slow negotiating stairs—apologetic
about not having a lift. But the apartment, when we reach it, is
worthwhile. Pleasant living room, grand piano, objects d'art, cases
of books in rich bindings—and a reception committee. Here is
Otto (who didn't come down because of his artificial leg)[1] and his
cousin, Carl, and the respective wives, Nora and Maria, and Carl's
daughter, Frida—tall, dark, pretty. It was one of the most interesting
conversations I have ever had. We had immediately a feeling of family
relationship, particularly with and through Maria, who is tall, good-
looking, accomplished, kind—and some more nice things. Most of
the conversation was in German, but we had instantaneous breaks,
from time to time, into English, French and Italian. They were all more*

or less competent in English in an awkward sort of way. When I got stuck in German they would say, "Say it in English." And it would usually go over. I got on rather well with the German. The words came somehow—from somewhere. Some I had never used before.... [The people] were lovely—just lovely. They had been waiting, I suppose, for an hour or so. I had been indefinite about the time of my prospective arrival. They had ready what would in England have been tea but was here coffee. And nice cake, for which I was thankful, for I had gone on without lunch.... Carl has a sister, Sofie, living in Heidelberg....

When at last I tore myself away they all came downstairs to see me off.... And now I am here in Venice. I must write a letter to Otto.

Venice. April 3, 1938

That was a very wonderful experience, those few hours in Venice. It is difficult, if possible, to resist the tendency to romance and poetization (see how it affects my choice of words). It is an extraordinary place. Nothing else like it in the world. Holland?—Naah!

Venice is real. It is wonderful—just as wonderful as if it were a dream—more so. I don't need to give a description of it. You have read and heard them. Now you can believe them.

Bolzano, Italy. Evening, April 3, 1938

I must be careful. Something seems to have happened in the last half hour to put me in a bad humour.... The hotel man, Herr Held, to whom I had come with an introduction from his son, a clerk in the Continentale in Naples, had given me a room at the maximum price. I thought he was trying to gyp me. I have put up with one gouge after another all day. It seems as if they are just waiting for "us Americans" (no "we Americans" the way I feel at the moment).

For here we are in Heinieland. It is near the border; it was once Austria. Every word I hear around me here in the ristorante of the hotel is German. The people are real Germans (listen to them "wunderbar"-ing around here).

Now I must be careful and not be biased, but for the moment my feeling is that these are a hateable and hateful people. The waitresses are a darker, smaller lot—real Austrians. I feel no repugnance toward them.... But I must be careful. (I have just insisted to the waitress on the English pronunciation of "butter." Really I must snap out of this or I shall find myself prejudiced.) But really I think there is something infectious about these people. It is their nature to treat, and be treated, rough. I am making them take it and like it. I eat my salad with my fingers, French style. (I hope it is not German style. I don't know.) I do all my ordering in English.... But just you watch. Butter won't melt in my mouth tomorrow. The waitress has been sweet—fallen in with my course English ways—pulls out her best broken English in a gentle effort to please. Oh damn! And to-morrow I shall be in Heinie.

Bolzano. Next morning, April 4, 1938
I am beginning to suspect that you have a certain usefulness, O Journal, like the fleas on a dog—to keep him from broodin' on bein' a dog. Should I have added that last, after the dash? Was it, O Reader, forcing the obvious? It is a choice between paying the reader a passing compliment and underestimating his breadth of knowledge.

And while I am at it, may I expatiate for a moment upon the advantages of this kind of life. A tramp has his pleasures. Think of the things he doesn't have to do. And here am I with my pack in the back of the car instead of in a red handkerchief on a stick. I can stop at Innsbruck and give them the time to do my laundry, or I can, like a tramp, go on with it as it is.... I have a wonderful privilege on this rapid trip, with its blur of impressions, to take in, as by a moving picture, in a few days, the development, architecturally and culturally of a large section of the human race—from mud hut of Egypt—or to go back even farther—from the peripatetic tent of some roaming Arab of the desert—to Greek and Roman case. Also the blossoming out, all along the line, into shrine and temple and mosque and cathedral and castle.

Wegenast picked up two German men, living in Italy near Bolzano.

An der Grenze [at the boundary between Italy and Austria].
April 4, 1938
One was pretty well soused.... Between the two of them talking freely I got quite an insight into local racial matters. They were both Germans.... All this northern corner of Italy—what we used to read about during the War as the Upper Adige—was predominantly German. But the Germans are having a hard time of it. There was considerable unemployment. The wages were miserable—four or five

lire a day (25 cents). No one could get a public position, for example as roadsweeper, unless he had an Italian education. And the taxes were terrible. The Germans would no doubt step in some day and take the country over again, anyway not that Austria had been taken over. There certainly is no love lost between the Germans and Italians as races.

At the boundary between Italy and Austria he picked up another passenger, a young Bavarian who was on his way to Munich. They crossed the border separately and then rejoined each other. Arriving in Innsbruck, Wegenast learned that Hitler was to give a speech to the Austrians, and a huge parade was planned. The plebiscite vote for union with Germany was to be on April 10. Wegenast decided to stay in Innsbruck.

Innsbruck, Austria. Evening April 4, 1938

A room? How long do I want to stay? One day only. Yes, they can give me a room but only till noon. You know Der Fuehrer is coming. There will be a big crowd, etc. [Wegenast was then told the next day that Hitler would stay in that very hotel, but he managed to stay on at the hotel.] So! The Fuehrer is going to be right here. So here I was with a seat in front of the balcony for the big show, literally the balcony of my window fronting the square. Hitler had a suite on the corner. By the way, he is freely spoken of as just "Hitler" or just "Der Hitler," though of course in polite conversation it is "Herr Hitler" or preferably "Der Fuehrer."

I find I can get along well enough with my German. And it is not necessary to hunt for the High German word if the Pennsylvania Dutch expression is at hand. It is only a matter of language, but if he condescends to use the vernacular that is nice and köflich (courtly) of him. These Americans are so democratic anyway. For what we call in America "Pennsylvania Dutch" is just ordinary vernacular in Germany—all of it. That is to say Pennsylvania Dutch expressions are not current in every part of Germany, but they are all current in some part. The word kriegen, to get, which seems so terribly necessary to the Englishman, is, I believe, current everywhere in Germany, except in polite society. There you have to use the equivalent of "obtain," or "acquire," or "seize" or "catch."... The Pennsylvania Dutch pronunciations are all current also—somewhere—ebbes for etwas, kee for kein, nix for nichts,[2] etc. And they have brought back into use the old (Swabian wasn't it?) Zwo instead of Zwei for telephoning purposes, because it is not so easily mistaken for drei.[3]... There isn't so much of the Swiss vernacular or pronunciation in America. Why?

Innsbruck. April 5, 1938
My Bavarian turned up again just as I had got the arrangement made for the room. He explained that he had gone to some state institution where fellows like him could spend the night.... I invited him up to my room. It was going to be an advantage to me to have him to talk with while watching the show. And it was a show—all the more effective for being unrehearsed—if that is putting it correctly, for there was not lacking the element of design or plan.

All afternoon bodies of men in uniform came pouring into the town, and people from the surrounding country, many in their striking Tyrolese costumes (though here, as elsewhere, the local costumes are giving way). As the solders with their bands arrived they marched into the square in front of the hotel.... Some came in civilian clothes and carried suitcases, probably containing uniforms or regalia. Many were regular troops with full equipment. There were, for example, as my Bavarian afterwards explained,

A)   the S.S., or Schutz-Staffel;
B)   the S.A., or Sturm Abteilung;
C)   the Deutsches Landes Polizei;
D)   the N.S.K.K. or motorized S.A.,

And so on—

Each with its own distinctive colour and uniform; mostly with full field equipment.

Then there were civil organizations (they allow them if they are favourable to Hitler); the Austrian Bundesheer, the Hitler Jugend, the B.D.M. (Bund Deutschen Mädchen) [possibly should read Bund Deutscher Mädel, or League of German Girls], and so on. The uniform of the various bodies had more significance to the local people than they had to me. There were of course German soldiers, those who had over-powered Austria and were now in effect occupying it. The pro-German element of the population of course regarded them as redeemers. The rest had to pretend so to regard them. Then there were the Austrian troops which had turned, or been switched over ("Been switched" is rather good in that connection). And of course there were the local "Partie" organization, which had been working for just this.

They marched, marched, marched. When they didn't have a band they sang—sometimes in two or three parts. They must have rehearsed that. That is to say, the civil organizations sang. I don't think any of the soldiers did. They were efficiently silent except for the resounding tramp of their hobnailed boots.

The constitution of a German band deserves some description. I am not sure that I observed carefully enough to be altogether exact; but there are certain outstanding features: In the first rank of course slide trombones. Then the horns and basses, including baritones or euphoniums. Then the clarinets and piccolos—plenty of them— because they strive for the tittley-tum effect of a little German band. But there is something I had never seen before, viz. a series—two or three or four, according to the size of the band—of brass instruments bringing up the rear. They seemed to be of the rank of baritone. They may have been what used to be called "bombardion." I could not tell whether they were E♭ or B♭. They seemed to be between.

The bells of the brass instruments did not have much flare. They were like our bugles. Last of all they usually had a "glockenspiel." The boy usually knew his stuff. He had, of course, to play without music. The whole band often did that. And those boys could march and play both at one time.

I haven't mentioned the drums. They came before the last of the brass. And there is something to be said about the drums that I do not know how to say. They were, first of all, extraordinarily exact. In fact the whole band played with extraordinary Tackt. But there was something more—especially about the method of drumming. It had an effect similar to that of the drumming of savages in Africa who are able to communicate this for hundreds of miles, over impenetrable forests. There was a curious affinity between the rhythm of the drums and the sound of the marching with hob-nailed boots. This was something which had been carefully cultivated. Its effect was an incitement to savagery. It vibrated, pulsated, throbbed—it <u>got</u> you.

At noon the public began to take places on the sidewalks for the performance they knew would not take place before six o'clock for it was then Hitler was to arrive. He was to speak at a hall at eight. But his arrival there was to be a review of the marching bodies, soldiers, police and civilian organizations.

Presently lines of soldiers were placed shoulder to shoulder along the curb to control the crowd. There was, of course, the odd argument. An old woman would be unable to understand why she could not go through the line of soldiers to her daughter behind them. When the soldiers couldn't do anything else they would shuttle them from one side of the street to the other.

But these were essentially an orderly people. They take readily to direction. The police never expect resistance—and are, on that account I suppose, in a position to be more human—if they feel like it. And after all why shouldn't they, their mothers and sisters are in the crowd. These people stood there in ever denser numbers below my window and around the square and in every direction for the whole afternoon. Things would happen; bands would play, bodies would march, but they were waiting for one thing only.

At last, near six o'clock, a cry goes up. But it is a false alarm. There are two or three more false alarms. Then, finally, there <u>was</u> a cry. <u>Can</u> these people yell? I suppose they get practice yodeling across one mountain to another. From then on it was more or less pandemonium every minute. Even the silences were pan demoniac. For these people are nothing if not orderly inter se. The demoniac streak is in the mass. We often say "individually the Germans.... etc." Nothing more true. But—yes <u>but</u>. Anyway their silences are as intense as their noise. At the loudest moment they could break unto absolute silence if there were occasion for it—if for example the Fuehrer began to talk. And they <u>sang</u>—sang. Throughout the afternoon they had sung along with songs like "Today we have Germany and tomorrow we shall have the whole world." Although the meaning is equivocal; it may mean or imply any one of several things. It is the same with the song, "Deutschland Uber Alles!" That song is rather innocuous. "Deutschland über Alles," by the way, goes to the tone of the former Austrian National Anthem—"Gott Behüte Franz den Kaiser" that is to say the Austrian hymn before the war. It must be a shock to the Austrians to hear the tune once more brought in by the Germans.

But nevertheless there is something of an implication of a possible deeper meaning. The Germans are given to that. Hitler is a past master of the extra-verbal innuendo. The song wants them to stick to German women, German wine, etc. But the title suggests not German, but German over everything. Of course the whole idea is to play up the theory that the Germans and Austrians were really all one and that their cruel enemies had been keeping them apart. It was Adolf Hitler that had stood up to these enemies and told them where they were getting off at. Note the appeal to the German women by rooting for Deutsche Frauen. *Is there any other nationality of women that would fall for that? Would French or an English woman wish to herd or be herded in that fashion? "Let's keep our men for ourselves." And it seems altogether likely that the anti-Jewish program owes much of its force to the singing of this hymn of implied hate.*

The scene below me, to use the trite phrase, rather beggars description. More particularly the sound is something ultra-Anglo-Saxon. It has something of the nature of the organized cheering at a great rugby game—only it is not organized—except in the sense that it organizes itself—a sort of spontaneous regimentation. For it would seem that the German not only submits to regimentation but he, as it were, crystallizes into it. As the atoms fly together to constitute molecules, so the Teutonic particles fly together true to a certain law. Hitler may at most have supplied a catalyst. The spontaneity is shown by the organized cries of the mob. Here are some of them. "Dear Leader, come out"—this over and over again. Here are some more. "We want to see the Leader." "Victory, hail"—over and over. "One people, one Kingdom, one Leader." "We now have a Leader."

An American boy, (United Statesan or Canadian, i.e., British Canadian) if he has an afternoon off, is likely to take down his fishing pole and hunt up a chum to go fishing. Not so the German boy. He would get together a dozen or twenty other boys and they would march, in rank and file and sing.[4] That is the German boy's idea of a good time. And as likely as not they would sing in harmony. And there would arise by some method a leader—a Fuehrer. There is a whole world of ethnological disquisition in the disgust which an English boy would have for this last—singing in harmony. If any fellow tried that in a gang of Anglo-Saxon boys, except, perhaps, for devilment around a camp fire at night, the rest of the gang would strangle him. And properly so, in the opinion of the prejudiced observer. It is basic. It goes to the root of all this ghastly cleavage in the world today. And if a naïve German father should read these lines he wouldn't know what it was all about. Now shouldn't his son sing an alto or a tenor? Doesn't it sound nice? Now why doesn't some faithful, industrious German Teufelsdroeck [perhaps should read Teufelsdreck, or devil's dung] take this ethnological problem in hand and elucidate it? What sort of barbarians are these Anglo-Saxons that they don't appreciate harmony? I'll bet ten to one he doesn't get it. I'll give him a lead: Why

*do Jewish law students go around in threes or fours, never in twos?
That ought to start him on something.*

*10:30 at night. This is tremendous, <u>kolossal</u>. I have never seen or
imagined anything like it before—shall never again. No amount of
stage-management could have produced all of this result. Its nature
is illustrated by something I saw late this afternoon. A dog, of the
Scotch wire-haired type—obviously of a kind not lacking in natural
courage—ran across the square. It was not being chased; but one
could see that it was really terrified at the manifestation of sheer
animal force in the cries of that crowd.*

*Night. The Fuehrer has made his speech. There have been the
usual presentations and introductions. The proceedings have been
broadcast from the hall to the crowds in the streets. There was no
diminution of the enthusiasm. The square to the left of my balcony
is packed farther than I can see. On my right and below me a dense
mass of humanity of all grades and classes. They want once more
to see and hear the Fuehrer. They will not be denied. It is announced
through the loud speakers that the Fuehrer will speak. A great cry
goes up. He speaks. He is a consummate mover of men. Every
sentence is weighed with approbation-drawing force. For every
sentence he draws a thunderous roar of acquiescence. Only two or
three minutes, but it would be enough to live a life for—many lives.*[5]

*This could not happen in England or in America—certainly not
in France. The people would not throw themselves into it like this....
Where is this heading?*

*I think Hitler is the best speaker—that is to say, the most
effective speaker, I have ever heard—I would not call him an orator;
he does not orate. Like Marc Anthony in Shakespeare he speaks
"right on"... every sentence counts—and usually gets applause.
But about every third or fourth sentence comes with a tremendous
punch. He reminds you of a black-smith. He is dynamic. His voice is
something like that of the late Sir Robert Borden's.*[6] *It has a boom
like distant thunder. He has a good voice but he abuses it by letting
it rise in his climaxes to the point where it cracks. He yells. But it
is what he says that counts. In the light of fuller knowledge than
his auditors have, or than he has himself perhaps, what he says is
something of clap-trap. But under the circumstances as he and his
hearers see them, including the character and outlook of the German
people, what he says is logical and sensible.*

Next morning, about 9:00 a.m. [April 6]

The excitement bids fair to start all over again. The crowd is not so large but it is already as vociferous. It wants to see the Fuehrer, who is probably having his breakfast. I ought to get mine. Last night it was 1:30 before I got any dinner. I got in about 11:30 but the tired waiters were overwhelmed. The place was full of officers. A few had ladies. These officers will stand studying. I have been looking them over since they began to crowd in last night—I mean the night before.

The officers are on the whole a rather prepossessing lot. There is one man six feet from me as I write in the breakfast room who bulges out at the hips like the other sex. His neck goes straight up behind—even tapers a bit. The plane of the back of his neck produced upward would not take long in meeting the production of the plane of his forehead. This fellow seems to have the makings of a perfect Prussian. But you can't tell by appearances. This fellow's wife may henpeck him. He may have a little daughter who adores him. He is very decent with his orderly.

I ought, indeed, I think, to observe that while there is much heel-clicking and saluting and precision there is an underground of what seems to be warm comradeship, not only between those of the same rank, but as between upper and lower. There does not seem to be any lick-spittling. After the cold salute and "Heil Hitler" the warm handshake and immediate ease. I suspect there is some of this also between officers and ranks, as it was in the case of the Canadians and United States.

As the time approaches for the Fuehrer to take his train the crowd gets denser both outside and inside the hotel. An expectant little crowd collects in the entrance foyer of the hotel. I stand around amongst them by the hall porter's desk. There is a variety in the personages. There are some women from the country with their children dressed their best—not exactly peasants but working people from outside the city. There is a family dressed in Tyrolese costume. They are all waiting for the Fuehrer to come through—to see him, and (if the great good fortune should befall them) to shake his hand. He comes, simply, like any other guest, on his way to the train. They crowd around him and shake hands. I could have done so. He is gracious and a little shy. This is the man who put to death, without a trial, one does not know how many Germans and is holding without trial Niemoeller[7] and Schuschnigg,[8] and one does not know how many more. The same bald porter who obsequiously licked stamps for my postcards, is now fussing over the Fuehrer's baggage in front of the hotel.

And the Germans here don't think much of the Italians. I sent out some laundry by the maid. I hadn't made a list. Afterwards I told her perhaps I should have done so. She assured me I would get every piece back. I said I was confident I would. I said after all one was amongst Germans, not Italians. Her face lit up, not with surprise but with pleasure that I, a stranger, should know things like that.

Innsbruck. Noon, April 6, 1938

This is getting a bit spooky. My Bavarian disappeared late yesterday afternoon. He had spent most of the day in my room where I had made him welcome. He was glad to see the show from my window and I was glad to have him to talk to. I didn't know how he would get along about getting in and out of the hotel. The management had given me a special card with which to get in and out of the door. I haven't had to use it; but no doubt they were taking extra precautions. I know, because about 7:20 this morning I was awakened out of my much needed sleep by a knock on the door. I admitted a man in civilian clothing who said he represented the "Pass Control." He wanted to see my passport. I gave him first my identification as [King's Counsel], then my passport. I asked him to what I was indebted for his interest in me. He explained that the Fuehrer Adolf Hitler was in this hotel and they had to be extra careful. I told him I thought it was wise and the interview ended. He apparently did not notice the hat and coat and knapsack of my Bavarian, who had not returned. He was not around yet at one o'clock. I didn't want to say anything to the hotel people for they might blame me for letting him in. I'll bet he was taken up by the police. His camera, a good one, is in my room too.

10 o'clock in the evening. Throughout the afternoon I got more and more worried about the boy. I hesitated to tell the hotel people about him for fear they would hold me accountable. Still it was a responsibility to let time go on without saying anything. I made several efforts to see Mr. Ambord[9] but at his office they were quite fishy about where he was or when he would be in. After four o'clock I got the porter to try to get him at his house. After more delay word came that he was now at his office. I told the story. He was quite understanding. While I was talking to Mr. Ambord it occurred to me that shortly before his disappearance the Bavarian had come in to

the room puffing after having run up three flights of stairs. He said
he had a weak heart—a family defect. I wondered if he had had a
seizure and was in a hospital, or dead.

Mr. Ambord advised telling the manager of the hotel. I did so.
He said he would get in touch with the police, which he did. Shortly
after I came into the hotel after a few minutes' absence and he told
me the police had got the things and that the boy had been here too
but had done away again and was now at the police station. I could
see him there. He had been under arrest but was free now. I went
to the police station, and after some search found him in the room
of an officer. He was apparently ill at ease (Why wouldn't he be?).
The officer—and the boy himself—said there was to be a "Control,"
which, they explained, was an investigation. It was to proceed at
once. I asked whether I could stay for it. The officer said it was
not necessary. He meant he didn't want me. The boy also seemed
against me staying. The officer said I could come back in half an
hour. The boy said he would come to the hotel when he was through.
He hasn't come.

Next morning, the 7th April
I put in the whole day at Innsbruck yesterday one way and another.
I suppose it was a matter of trying to locate the Bavarian whom I
never saw again.

This morning things had got back to normal. Across the street
a fruit-barrow man was doing business again. I bought some blood
oranges. He said now that they were going to be part of Germany
oranges would be dearer and harder to get. When I mentioned
Canada he said that was where the good apples came from.

Towards noon, the excitement had pretty well died down and
pretty well the last of the officers had mounted their high-powered
cars and shot off.

Later—Outside Germany
Now this is later and outside the land of the Teutons. You
understood, of course, dear reader, why one didn't speak out about
certain things. But do not misunderstand. Orally one could be pretty
free and frank. I was quite certain that I could have expressed
myself quite freely and disrespectfully about all I saw and heard at
Innsbruck without incurring anything serious. Of course if I had got on
a soap-box on the street ... they would have stopped me. But it was

quite obvious that they did not expect me to be bound by the same inhibitions that kept them from talking. I was an Ausländer.[10] *That was different. Moreover I was an* Englischer, *and they are certainly different. Those guys talk about anything. (Englischer includes the Amerikaner.) Let them talk their heads off. They are tourists. We need them. I could have talked quite freely. But write it down?—I figured that was different. Anyway I wouldn't trust the German post office with what I thought. So I stored it up. And as I go along I shall probably spill some of it from time to time.*

Rottweil, Germany. Evening, April 7, 1938

This forenoon, after leaving Innsbruck, I came to a little Tyrolese village of Haiming.... A little farther on, about Imst, I picked up a neatly dressed, bare-headed, black-haired young man without baggage. His name turned out later to be Josef Kobi. The young man first described himself as a "Hungarian." He had been born in Augsburg, Germany. He had a brother and sister still living there. His mother had been German. His father had been killed in the war. The boy had been declared by the authorities to be staatenlos *i.e., a man without nationality, and he had a passport as such—which was a new idea to me. He said he had never clearly understood why he could not be German, but it seemed his blood was not pure enough. I thought possibly he might be Jewish, but he did not look it. His idea was to work himself as far west as he could—to Strasbourg if possible; for his father had formerly worked there. He was hopeful if he got into France he could get a new start. There had been no future for him in Germany and now there was none in Austria, where he had been with a sister. As we drove along he guardedly evinced his lack of sympathy with German policy. He joined me in depreciating the result of the vote to be taken the following Sunday. The people could, of course, do nothing else but vote yes, but that did not mean that they were all in accord.*

In the village through which we passed, efforts were being made to decorate for the great event. Loads of evergreens were being brought in from the forests. The Swastika flag was everywhere. These flags, by the way, were I think not bought by the people who displayed them. They were supplied by the authorities. The display of a flag by a villager did not mean ... that he had gone out and spent his own good money for it. It might mean, in Innsbruck that someone had gone round selling flags and he had been afraid to refuse to buy one. But in Innsbruck I saw a truck going through the crowds and throwing handfuls, twenty at a time, of Swastika flags into the crowds. The truck might have been Austrian but the inspiration would be from the propaganda department of the German government.

As we drove along we would come across groups of children constituting, so it seemed, the local school population, practicing marching in procession. Sometimes they sang as they marched. Others had more or less rudimentary bands to play for them. In every case some earnest-looking man or woman was in command. But the rank and file did not show much enthusiasm. I fancy the Austrians had got out of the way of being military. But presently we came across a large autobus in which a body of marchers had obviously come, and I learned from my passenger, Kobi, that in some cases, at least, these marchers had been sent in probably from Germany. It was apparently part of the business of the propaganda department to see that there was marching in every locality, and if the locals could or did not supply the demand it had to be supplied from outside.

There will be a new lot of tourist literature out now, I suppose [with respect to visiting the Tyrol district and Austria generally]. They are clever at rubbing people the right way. The present German tourist literature is significantly reticent about political and governmental matters, and contains none of the fulsome allusions with which everyone in Germany licks the boots of those now in power. Someone has had the sense to censor the literature for foreign consumption. In other words, the Germans know how unpopular they are. It is indeed one of the ideas with which they lash themselves into patriotic jury. Nobody loves me; I'll go out in the garden and eat worms.

It must have been nearly two before we stopped at St. Anton for a lunch, which I asked my passenger to share with me. Some military trucks transporting German soldiers, which we had alternately passed and been passed by during the forenoon, were just ready to leave as we drove up. They were a heavy-set and rather surly bunch, but civil enough. The German soldier seems to have been told by someone that foreign travelers are not to be treated like other civilians so he is darn civil—"damn civil" might be better. That is not saying there are not some decent inoffensive fellows amongst them. Anyway, there is nothing like all of the old arrogance in the relationship of superior to inferior in Germany. The war and its aftermath took an awful lot of that out of them. And, of course,

*a house painter must be a bit hard to take as a national demi-god.
It might indeed turn out that the house-painter feature may save
Germany for the world. It may call into being the rude, elementary
beginnings of a sense of humor. You could hardly go into spasms
of patriotic fervour over a house-painter without taking a picture of
yourself out of the corner of your eye—not if you were a German
aristocrat. It is the fructification of German aristocracy and autocracy.
It is possible even, to regard it as a triumph of democracy. And there
must be for the Heinie officer many a bitter recollection of eating dirt
in the last ten years.*

*But Kobi and I are enjoying our lunch on a table covered with
red chequered cloth in the sunshine before the hotel. It is really a
little cool but it is a relief to have weather approximately spring like.
I get Kobi to go into a nearby shop to see if they will let him have
a copy of the printed display card announcing that here one greets
with "Heil Hitler" instead of "Good Morning." But they have only the
one copy. I saw some in shops in Innsbruck. I suppose the itinerant
salesman is cashing in on patriotism and fear alike. I shall not soon
forget the words of the old tailor in Innsbruck this morning. I shall
not give his name, in case this might in some way get in circulation.
I went in to have him sew a button on my vest. He had pressed my
clothes yesterday. We got talking about things. I had remarked just
before entering his shop, four tiny girls marching on the sidewalk
in the rank and file and goose-stepping. The old man said: "Ja da
jubelin sie der Strasse mit dem Militär; aber daheim sitzen viele
und weinen"—"yes, here they jubilate on the street with the military
but at home many sit and weep." The worst of it is that they have
to juble in the streets and register enthusiasm while their hearts
are breaking. Where are all the people who were said at the lowest
estimate to constitute 33 percent, who supported Schuschnigg? How
is it going to end?*

*Towards evening we reached Lake Constance, at Bregens, where I had
still a choice of going into Germany or going into Switzerland. I have
been thinking aloud to my companion, who was plainly hoping I would
go on toward Strasbourg. I thought also of the difficulty of laying
in Swiss money and the disposing of what I had left. In the end, I
decided to pass up Switzerland and [go on into Germany on the way
to] Alsace. So, as night was coming down, we journeyed along the
German shore of Lake Constance, bearing to the north-west.*

At the German border, my passport was perfunctorily examined. There was no trouble whatsoever. No search. My car not opened. I had my identification card again. Kobi told me afterwards that the German official had asked him, after I had been passed, what a Kongarat eigentlich [King's Counsel] was. Kobi informed him that it was some considerable pumpkins.

Our way led through Tuttlington to Rottweil, where I had thought of spending the night. There was a hotel that was recommended to me, but at the hotel they said they had no room. I was sorry to leave the old feudal town, which I had not explored the last time I went through. But it was getting late and I did not know what other hotel to try, so I decided to push on to the Sulz-am-Neckar.

Sulz-am-Neckar, District of Rottweil, in Baden-Württemberg, Germany. Next Morning, April 8, 1938

We went on and reached Sulz on schedule time. The people at Sulz were waiting for us. The car was taken to a hotel garage and everything was jake. I told the hotelkeeper I would pay for Kobi's room but that otherwise I would take no responsibility for him as I had only picked him up on the road.

Sulz is deserving of a little notice. It has been very much improved since I was here last. And N.B. the improvement has not been all in the last five years—indeed I would say very little of it.

So what? So this: Nazism and Hitlerism are the result, and not the cause, of revival in Germany. The enormous headway which Germany is making was on the way before Hitler ever came on the scene. I recall now that when I was through here in 1921 there were large construction projects in progress in this valley of the Neckar. I did not know the meaning of them until I saw in the Saturday Evening Post nearly two years later that the project was that of a canal system leading up from the Rhine into Switzerland. Similar works were in progress in other parts of Germany. The German people are kidding the world and themselves into thinking that it is Hitler that has ushered in the era of prosperity. Bunk. It was German industry and German readiness to work for whatever wages were obtainable that have put her where she is. And as the Germans saw themselves getting on their feet they began to feel their oats. The old military habits began to assert themselves once more—and in their old form of violence, but still very appreciably, as we now see them demonstrated.

Holzhausen, [near] Sulz-am-Neckar. April 8, 1938

It was nearing noon when at last I started up into the hills for Holzhausen, the native heath of the Wegenasts. The drive seemed shorter than I remembered it [from earlier trips to the area]. I had hardly started up the incline when I overtook a party of eight or ten little girls, from eight to twelve years.[11]... Thus we went up the hill. I asked them if they were from Holzhausen. They said they were from Austria. They were there for Erholung (recreation). They were staying in Holzhausen.... They were a contingent of children who have been hauled from Austria to Germany, reciprocally for others taken from Germany to Austria. It is a new idea which is being called in by way of adding an extra sob-touch to the voting campaign—also the old "Gleichschaltung" stuff. These girls are much smaller than any we had seen in the Tyrol village yesterday. Their right place was very obviously with their mothers. But that is also part of the idea. The children are taught that their first duty is to the Staat. The parents are O.K. so long as they gleichschalt (fall in)—"ride along" as the Americans would say. That is the great thing in Germany, ride along. Don't have any independent or individual ideas that are not agreeable to everyone else. In Germany the greatest public joke is the idea of "parliamentarizing."

Wegenast quickly located Carl Wegenast. That day he visited a number of other Wegenasts and unravelled some of his personal genealogy, before returning to Sulz for the night.

Kobi had begged in the morning to be taken along to Holzhausen but I refused. When I got back to Sulz he was still there. The landlord had given him some lunch and I had him in for dinner again and arranged for a room for him overnight. The landlord charged a little less for him than for me. I don't think the boy had a cent, although he had not given me the impression at first that he was completely strapped.

In the evening, Wegenast saw a poster near the hotel. It read as follows:

Plebiscite and Great Germany Reichstag
Do you concur in the re-union of Austria with the German
Reich as consummated on the 13th March, 1938, and do
you vote for the ticket of our Leader?

Adolf Hitler

Yes   No

Kobi was quite interested and I think it was he who suggested that
we might get a copy of the poster itself by applying to the office of
the Hitler Youth, of which there would doubtless be one in Sulz. He
actually located the office and was at some pains to get the woman
in charge to go to the office with the key and look for the poster.
There were no copies left. They had all been utilized. He got several
others, however, to add to my collection.

At Freudenstadt he tried it once more. This time he succeeded.
He turned up with a rather prepossessing lot of Hitler boys who were
keen to help out this foreigner's search for the truth, and who, when
they saw my car were quite willing to make me one of themselves.
They found one of the posters and some other interesting ones, all of
which I have still by me. They were as fine a lot of boys as you could
wish to meet. I played the radio for them to their delight; and by way
of acknowledgement of their helpfulness (they quite understood
it was not a handout), I gave several of them Canadian nickels, of
which I had a quantity. I didn't, of course, have enough to go around,
but I left it to one particularly gentlemanly fellow to use his judgment
in making the distribution.

Kobi seemed pleased, not only at being able to do something
for me, but also because he appreciated my reasons for wanting
the poster. He knew perfectly what a farce this vote was going to
be. We had made a number of stabs about it as we drove along.
We were on common ground. How could anyone in his senses take
the thing seriously?

Think of R.B. Bennett[12] going to the country under these
circumstances: (For it would be a Tory Government). There would
be party committee rooms everywhere; but only one party. Every
other party would have been "liquidated." (Think of that! Wouldn't
you politicians like to see the other party completely liquidated.)
There would be plenty of campaign literature. All the literature would
be printed by the government. All the posters would be gotten out
and put up by the Government—by the young Conservatives. No
one would be allowed to say anything against the Government. If
he did he would, at best, be beaten with a bunch of umbrella rods
to be taught Toryism. And suspicion that he might vote against the
Government would be given to understand that they must keep
an eye on their parents and tell the authorities if they thought
there was any ground for suspicion that they might not be 100%
for the government. The mounted police, of whom there would be

tens of thousands all over the country, would investigate any case of suspected unfriendliness to the Government. There would be prosecutions for the crime of "Government-unfriendliness."

What utter nonsense. And a whole people of 75,000,000 people making it their business to go through with it. Talk about democracy, and a capacity for self-government. The tragedy of it is that nobody in Germany thinks of that ballot as funny. Perhaps "nobody" is a bit too strong for 75,000,000. And I must remember that Kobi saw through it. But hardly anybody—not one in twenty. I touched several people up on it. They either didn't know there was anything remarkable or they would remark, "Well, everyone knew how the vote would go." Passing up the crazy logic of this statement, it seems still an important inquiry <u>why</u> this statement should be correct—for obviously it is correct. There is one consideration that makes it less (or is it more?) serious. Everyone seems to agree that if Schuschnigg.... had conducted the plebiscite in Austria the ballot would have been similarly weighed down the other way. And I think there is still further; that there is general agreement that there is really a substantial majority of opinion in favour of union with Germany.

On the whole, it is the German <u>method</u> that the rest of the world cannot stomach.

Have seen a few good chickens in Austria—some White Leghorns, also Black Minorcas. Brown Leghorns seem to be still popular here. I saw hardly any Barred Rocks, no Wyandottes, unless one lot of Columbian Wyandottes which I took for Columbian Rocks.[13]

<u>Quite a while later</u>—now I have the real key to the mystery of the over 99 percent vote in favour of the Anschluss.[14] You know how a vote is taken in Anglo-Saxon countries. You go into the polling place. In front of you, behind a table, sits the Deputy Returning Officer, beside him sits the Poll-Clerk. One or the other of them asks your name. The poll-clerk runs over his list and finds it and checks it off. In the meantime the D.R.O. folds a ballot and initials it, and gives it to you. Then he points to a corner of the room curtained off and supplied with a desk and a pencil fastened to a string and says: "There's the place to vote." Suppose you say to the D.R.O, "I won't bother going over there; I'll mark my ballot right here." The D.R.O. will say, "No, I can't let you do that; you will have to go over there." That is our system. The German system is like it, even to the pencil on the string. But the German D.R.O. will say: "Over there is a place to

vote, but you can vote right here." And you do, or you are a marked man. I am told the D.R.O. makes a separate pile of the ballets that are marked behind the curtain. Oh, they will be honest enough in counting. The German would strain at dishonesty, but he swallows the camel of non-secrecy. Now you have it. The Englishman is out to make democracy work; if secrecy is necessary to make it work, by all means let's have secrecy. The German says: "Why should a man be afraid to show how he votes? If that stands in the way of democracy so much the worse for democracy." And I am giving the German the benefit of some doubts.[15]

Maison Rouge Hotel, Strasbourg, Alsace, France. April 9, 1938
Out of Germany! Hoorey! I am once more on the soil of France. What a relief! What an expansion of the lungs! There is something stifling over there. How can I explain it?

My poor friend, Kobi, fell by the way. It was this way: As far back as Sulz I had heard him say to a chance acquaintance at the hotel that for his passport he did not need a visa. There was some discussion in which I took part. The German officer was more deferential to me than to Kobi. He said he knew they would not let him into France without a visa. There was some talk about the boy's deserving consideration because his father had, after all, fought for Germany. The officer conceded to me that the boy might try it but it would be useless. I said, of course, I would take his word for it. He advised Kobi to see the French Consul on the German side, that, at Kehl. But it was now nearly noon. The office [Cook's] would be closed before we could get there. I was anxious to get over to Cook's for my mail and some money. I thought they would be closed on the Saturday afternoon. So I told Kobi I would have to go on without him. He begged me with a hunted look in his eyes. But I steeled myself. After all, I had kept him for two days and brought him to the border. That was surely enough for my share.

He said I had ways of helping myself and him. I suppose I did, but I was a stranger in a foreign country. I didn't know what I might get into. So I went off. I have been sorry ever since. I still see the bruised look in his eyes.

I suppose there are a good many of these fellows wandering around. They are outcasts for one reason or another. My Bavarian friend may have been one too. Apparently it is not enough to have a passport that is in order. The Bavarian had that. For it is not merely a matter of crossing borders. At any moment the police may pick you up if everything is not in order—perhaps even if it is. What a life!

Sarresbourg, France. Evening of April 9, 1938

A policeman recommended this hotel in Sarresbourg.... I really stopped here to ascertain whether there is any place near where there would be an Amish Church service tomorrow. I got a lot of information more or less correct from a red-faced, thick-set man in the wine room—which made me decide to stay here.

For the information was that the meeting house is right here, within a block of the hotel. And this is the meeting place of the Nafzigers of Hirschland as well as the Pelsys. The Pelsys are only about two miles out of here, at a farm called Muckenhof. I didn't remember that it was so near. I had got acquainted with them fifteen years ago when I was here.

Sarresbourg, France. April 10, 1938

I drove out to Muckenhof to see the Pelsys. I recognized the farm and drove in through the farmyard up to the house.... I was brought into the kitchen where Mr. Pelsy and the two boys were having supper.... We got to talking about the Amish here and in Canada. Here, of course, they dress like anyone else. But they remember some who came from America some years ago who wore the hooks and eyes. The older folks know there was such a custom once— also the custom as to beards. [Wegenast went to, and enjoyed the service at the meeting house later that day.]

Sarresbourg, France. April 11, 1938

Had an interesting chat with the pretty daughter of the hotel, and afterwards her mother. From them I learned the result of the elections in Germany yesterday. I told them about my day in Innsbruck.... They readily agreed that the situation as developed in Germany was "schrecklich" [dreadful]. One lived in fear—fear of another war, and the possibility of conquest by Germany.

What is the present situation in Alsace as regards the two languages? Does the Hitler campaign awaken any response in Alsace or Lorraine? (French may be the official language but at home the Germans speak German.) Then there are cross-currents like this: The labour union class, those who support the forty-hour week, *naturally support the Government, while the others see that there is at least this to be said for Hitlerism, that it gets people to work. But for the rest of the German polity, non, non, non. They know the difference between liberty and slavery. They have lived under Germany. They understand gleichschaltung.[16] They understand how one heaves a great sigh of relief immediately on crossing the border from Germany into France, and how one puts on the mantle of fear and furtiveness on crossing the other way.*

Of course, it comes down to a question of racial and personal make-up. If you are the kind of person who wants to go to a beer cellar at night and sing with your fellows in harmony, you will prefer to be with others of the same bent. If you like to take your excursion into the country in a company marching in rank and file and singing, well, you have to find others who like that kind of kameradschaft. If you like, on the contrary, to go fishing with a single companion or alone, you will be better off somewhere else than in Germany.

The French Government, on its part, seems to be pursuing a very wise policy in dealing with the German-speaking population of Alsace. It places them under no disability or embarrassment. It even broadcasts news and agricultural information in German. It is a free country.

Later, April 11, 1938

At the moment I am sitting at what appears to be the crest of a mountain pass. Many miles of mountain and valley lie before and below me. It is something like the Adirondacks but less wild, for some of the mountains have on their sides cultivated farms with splendid outbuildings. It has been a beautiful drive through copious forests of fir in natural state.

Wegenast travelled through French towns. His attention now became focused on French cathedrals, and he assessed their architecture against what he had read. He referred frequently to Stendhal's commentary on the subject. Wegenast's remarks about the cathedral at Dol serve as an example of his consuming interest in this subject.[17]

Dol, France. April 15, 1938

Have been looking forward to this for a long time; now that it has materialized it seems common-place enough. The Cathedral no doubt is wonderful, but it requires a mental effort to hold one's mind

*to an appreciation of the things for which it is said to be wonderful.
For I may as well be frank with you, my journal, and say that I realize
the church is wonderful because I am so told by those who ought
to know. Stendhal, for example, says: "The Cathedral of Dol seems
to me one of the most perfect works which Gothic architecture
can offer to our imagination." Elsewhere he says: "The impiety of
the eighteenth century has made us lose the faculty for building
churches. Well, when a provincial city has money and asks for a
church, copy that of Dol."*

*I am sorry to say that I must disagree with Stendhal, and, what
is worse, I must disagree with my own recollection of fifteen years
ago. I thought I had seen the six-inch granite columns rising all
along from the floor to the corners of the vault. They are not there.
I debated whether I was really in the Cathedral of Dol. A check-up
verified that. I went out to the car and read Stendhal again. Then
I went back into the church and looked at the pillars again. They were
not [in an isolated state].*

*At this point I am interrupting the chronological sequence. I am
taking out several pages which were wrong and inserting the
following, written at*[18]

Lisieux, France. April 20, 1938
*Thought I might as well go through Dol and see the Cathedral once
more and check over the description I had put down.*

*It is distressing to see how positive and that the same time
how wrong one can be. I had undertaken to correct Stendhal
and I thought I had carried away the correct impression. But with
the fairest and most honest intentions in the world I put down a
description which I find today was incorrect in certain particulars.*

*This, of course, is an example of the thing with which lawyers
and judges become so familiar, namely, the difficulty of getting even
honest witnesses to tell the truth.*

*Stendhal, of course, was wrong—quite wrong—in saying there
were pillars complètement isolée. I find, by the way, in a guide book
which I bought today, the same mistake repeated—unless I don't
understand French.*

*You can take it from me that after looking at it four times, three
times on Friday and again once today, and after discussing it all
on Friday with a priest who kindly came into the church with me for*

that purposes, I find no isolated column or columns.... Anyway, an infinite capacity for taking pains (and making blunders) can make for ultimate truthfulness, at least. But it takes the conceit out of one.

I don't suppose you care a fig, Journal, what the pillars are actually like, but, since so much has been said, let me give the following from close personal observations and drawings made on the spot. [A drawing and a three-page description of the columns follow.]

Paris, France. April 25, 1938

Late this afternoon I went out to Notre Dame. It is a bit ridiculous to drive all over the country to see all the little churches and pass this, perhaps the greatest of them all. The evening was lovely.... On the green sward west of the church the birds which are the equivalent of robins were disporting themselves.

About Paris there does not seem to be anything to write. It is a puzzle to drive a car but not as bad as in New York. The police are very decent. Their methods have improved greatly since I was here last. They don't gesticulate so much. And the cars don't use their horns as much.

After I came back from Notre Dame I pulled up in front of the Café de la Paix and ordered afternoon tea à l'Anglais. It was forth coming. I sat there for an hour or more seeing the current styles displayed by handsome ladies on the street. This could be very pleasant on afternoons like this.

[The visitor is] impressed, at least between four and five in the afternoon, with sidewalk cafes. There half the world sits four or five tables deep on the sidewalk taking a sip of something occasionally and watching the other half of the world go by.

I have heard a good deal of German talked near me in these cafes—some English too.

Wegenast drove through towns in Normandy, looking at churches and the countryside, before arriving at Rouen. While in Rouen, he continued to study architecture, and especially the architecture of the cathedral in this city. He then went on to Reims.

East of Reims, France. May 5, 1938

Stopped at the side of the road where a farmer had stopped at the end of his furrow with one of these double-shared plows.... I said I was from Canada and he at once fell in with his own knowledge that

*there one used a plow with only one share. His little boy of about
nine had just come along.... Mr. Nouvelet (the farmer's name) told
me they were having a hard time with their crops this spring for want
of rain. It is chalky soil and cannot stand drought. He showed me
some oats that had been sown before Easter and was just coming
through. He said it should be eight inches high now.*

*One thing led to another and N. told me he had been through
the whole War. I said then he could explain de quel direction sont
tombé les obus sur Reims? Yes, he could explain all that. He showed
me the high points to the north-east and east, about four or five
miles from where we stood, where the German batteries stood
which bombarded Reims. He himself spent most of the four years
at Verdun. His brother, after whom the boy was named, was killed
there. To my saying that there were also many Canadians in the
War he said he knew very well. He had had a comrade in the War
who was a French Canadian and who told him a lot about Canada.
It was a little hard to get away from him, he was so interested in
this traveler from Canada. I shook hands with him and the boy with
mutual expressions of good wishes.*

*A little further on some men were levelling a trench on the left side
of the road. It was a short piece left of a war trench. I did not see the
men at first, but when I climbed the bank of the trench I saw them. The
men told me this was just a little piece of trench left right beside the
road which they had neglected to fill sooner. Everything else had been
filled in so you could not see that the fields had ever been disturbed.*

Reims, France. May 5, 1938

*[Impressions of] Reims. Place to recall the War. Americans.
Cathedral. Organist—young. Siegfried Schmidt. Post cards.
R.C. Books. Sunshine. Destruction. Restoration. Beauty. Flying
Buttresses. New Organ. Not so Latin. Crickets.*

*In Reims you can still get a fairly graphic idea of the ravages of
the War. They rather feature it. American tourist trade I suppose. Not
that I have any objection. There ought to be places where trenches,
no man's land etc., could be preserved. Like, for example, this:
the Cathedral is still the poignant reminder of it all. It has been, or
is being, partially restored. But the beautiful windows which were
destroyed are now glazed in white. The mutilated pillars, the half
melted bells, the headless saints and prophets are mute witnesses to
the artistry of the Hun. The polite thing would have been to say "the*

artistry of War." People are so fond [of that expression] now—and they think it denotes wisdom and poise—of generalizing about "war" and deprecating the "injustices" of the Treaty of Versailles. Wholesale childishness and imbecility! I may have more to say about that.

When I went into the Cathedral I had the vanity to wish for a picture of myself and the car in front of it. I manoeuvred the car into the right position and looked for someone to take the snapshot. A young man was coming across the square toward me. I proffered my request. Yes, he was familiar with the taking of photographs.

Then we got talking. The fact that I was from Canada interested him. He had a great desire to go there and wanted me to advise him where would be the best place from which to sail. I told him about the C.P.R. and other lines and gave him a C.P.R. railway time table with addressees of steamship offices. But it was so difficult as to be almost impossible for him to get enough money. He was German. He had a position in Reims, but was not making enough money to enable him to accumulate the passage money. His people in Germany had money but would not be allowed to spend it on passage money. But he hoped in some way it could be done.

This young man's name was Siegfried [spelling by Wegenast changes later on] Schmidt. I hope I have not lost his address—no here it is: 9, Rue St. Nicaise, Reims (Marne), France.

This young man was one of those from whom I got the totality of impressions about Germany and the Germans which I am expressing from time to time. It is difficult to reconstruct the conversation and still more difficult to reconstruct the tones and innuendos which mean more than the words themselves. There was, for example, no surprise but understanding when I said that on my return home it was questionable where I should say I had been in Germany.

Notwithstanding so many items of destruction the Cathedral of Reims may yet compare for beauty with any church in the world.... Reims and its people do not appear so Latin. Have we got into the country of the Franks, who were Germanic?

Crickets are singing for joy in the sunshine.

I picked up a quantity of R.C. books and pamphlets here as to other churches. I may refer to them.

In all countries it is the village life, and, I should say, the farm life, that gives the country its character. Cities are pretty much alike. Cabarets and casinos pretty much also. Theatres are indistinguishable. The villagers and the farmers remain different.

City of Luxembourg. May 6, 1938

Arrived here after dark last night and am lodged at the Hotel Central Molitor (whatever that means). It is not much of a hotel. But we are now again in a district peopled by Germanics. Certain results follow. It is cleaner. You have more confidence in the bed sheets, the silverware, the floors—everything about the house....

Later I was in a little tobacco, newspaper and souvenir store near the hotel several times in the morning and struck up an acquaintance with the proprietor.

All the same, Journal, I may as well admit that it does give me a bit of a thrill to do as I did with a tobacconist—go into his store and find him reading a paper in German; I look at the paper while he is wrapping up my parcel, I ask him in French what the politics of the paper are; I continue the discussion in German, find it is a paper of the Rechts, *d.h. (i.e.) Catholic, but he does not agree with my suggestion that that means they are more German than French. He says they make no difference here. They slam Hitler because of his attitude to Catholics etc.—chatting along, in French and German alternately with a Luxembourger. It is a privilege and something to enjoy—if human communication is something to enjoy—and it is, if you ask me.*

In Luxembourg as in the other countries touching Germany on the west, the tendency is not to talk in German if you can help it—at all events not where there is a favourable impression to be made. Amongst intimates, in the home, in the beer cellar—probably in the church, German or Germanic may be all right, but in the restaurant, in the bank, even on the street, you don't want to pass for a German.

In the restaurant, you get better attention if you talk French. You are somebody. If a Germanic working-girl began to talk French her companions would say she was putting on airs. A French girl would think it low to talk German. That does not mean that there is not a race pride in the Germans. I suppose you would find a certain amount of that in a negro. That of course sounds bitter and relatively ill-bred. But the point is that that is the way it gets here. It is in the atmosphere. We are not in England—or even America.

The main thing in talking French in the ordinary commerce, as in shops, restaurants, etc., is to use a light sing-song tone which would be considered crazy in America. It is something like you would talk to a tiny tot of two years of age. It is like some Americans say

"All rightie" or "Nightie-nightie"—the same idea. It shows you are so pleased that you are inclined to be playful. It gets, of course, to be pure technique on the part of the shop keepers. They do it automatically. But it is expected—like "Thank you so much." The important thing is not so much what you say as your attitude.

Had lunch at a patisserie. *Bought a little bunch of violets from a little girl who prattled to me in German and said her father had picked them.*

But I have been holding back from the very difficult tasks of recording something of the beauty and charm of the afternoon which followed my stop in the City of Luxembourg. It would be pleasant to stay right there. The City has a charm all its own. For one thing the people have an air of well-being and satisfaction that is striking on a German face. For they are mostly German though they are all taught French and regard it as the polite language. They have, indeed, three languages—the Luxembourg, the High German and the French. The Luxembourg is a dialect of German, as Dutch and English are. But that does not mean that a person who speaks High German can speak or understand Luxembourg, any more than Dutch or English.

I am on my way to find Peter Nafziger whose name and address I have from his brother Christian Nafziger of Lowville, N.Y. He is to be found at Lauterborn Mühle (Mill), bei Echternach.... At the place which I afterwards found to be Valper there was only one house by the side of the road. It was well painted and looked like a flourishing country inn. But it wasn't, as I found out on stopping to enquire. It was the abode of a pensioned road worker and his efficient wife. They cheerfully furnished information. Yes, they knew Peter Nafziger. Lauterborn Mühle was only a few kilometres farther on. Nafziger and his family were "nette Leute" (nice people). They held strictly to their religion [Mennonite].... But they were good people.

Hotel des Ardennes, Echternach, Luxembourg.[19] May 9, 1938
The last three days have been so full of worth-whileness that I despair, mon Journal, of getting down anything adequate about it. I had expected to spend a night here and then go on. Instead I have spent three nights with Peter Nafziger. This visit will be among the most memorable events of my whole journey. It started late on Friday afternoon when I drove down the steep incline into Lauterborn Mill

and explained to Herr Nafziger the circumstances that had brought me to call on him, namely, that his brother in Lowville, N.Y. had mentioned in a letter that he had a brother at Lauterborn, Mühle, etc.

They were very much alike, the three brothers, Joseph, Peter and Christian. The same sweet, whimsical strength of character. Good business men and house-keepers, kind but not too indulgent fathers, and firmly grounded in religious faith and practice, and, generally, men of poise and practical sense. It would be interesting to know their parents.... [Peter has three children at home]— Joseph, Pierre and Mina.

Mina is a big, sunny, practical girl with an infusion of her father's whimsicality but a real verve which the French would call esprit. A peasant girl, but one of whom I was not ashamed when I took her and her two brothers into the Palace Hotel at Mondorf-les-Bains yesterday afternoon for afternoon tea in English style.

One thing has just led to another in the most delightful fashion for the three days, without any expectation, on my part, of being there even for a single meal.

They are very nicely equipped with a bathroom, or more, and electric light from their own power. Mina is an excellent cook. For supper, I had trout, just fished out of the fountain and fried. Then, of course, meat and vegetables. Yes, there was soup first and cake and coffee afterward.

In the discussion of Mennonites and Amish (the two terms seem to be synonymous here) they produced a calendar containing a list of all the congregations and their preachers in Germany and France and Switzerland—also in Poland. (In Russia they seem to have been rooted out; or perhaps it is not considered good policy to give the names there.) In this calendar, I see that my host is the preacher for this Gemeinde (congregation or parish).

On Saturday afternoon, while we were in the house which serves as place of meeting for his congregation, what does the old gentleman do but arrange that there would be a service the next day; because he sensed (nothing whatsoever was said about it before or after) that I would like to see them in meeting. On Saturday, the old gentleman had dropped everything and gone out of his daily round to go out with young Peter and me on a drive around the country.

Then yesterday Mina and the two boys and I took the afternoon to visit Luxembourg and Mondorf-les-Bains, and come back by way of the valley of the Moselle.

The meetings are held in the front room on the right of the door. It is simply the front room of the farm house. I think I understand perfectly the objection of some of the Amish in America to meeting in meeting-houses. But here in their original home, the Amish meet in houses because the congregations are too small to justify the expense of a meeting-house. And, of course, in a case like this, it is no trouble at all to the people in the house. It saves them the trouble of going elsewhere.

Then we got into politics. They got me to express my views or rather the views of the people in America on German politics. It was obvious that they all agreed except the old gentleman. He had, I think, a blood thicker-than-water tenderness for the German people and their way of doing, but he put it this way: "What is the use of policies anyway?" That is the traditional Mennonite attitude—of taking no part in the government, but being obedient citizens. That, of course, falls in with Hitler's ideas. But the rest ... were right up on the bit against Hitler and all his works. Young Pierre was right with them too.

The best of things have to come to an end. I am quite sure the Nafzigers joined in my regret at parting this morning. We have grown to be warm friends. I shall never forget their kindness. I am now intending to take a trip for the day into the hill country north and west of Echternach and then perhaps to return to Echternach to cross the border into Germany.

Hotel des Ardennes, Echternach, Luxembourg. May 10, 1938

Forenoon. Came back here for the night.... As I have already observed about the people of the City of Luxembourg, these in Echternach also have that distinct air of well-being. They show on their faces the lack of concern with taxing themselves to keep up an army. There is an army—of volunteers. Membership in it is considered something like a joke. Of course, there have to be technical guards at the frontiers—or rather—at the German and French frontiers. There is no customs duty between Luxembourg and Belgium and, I believe, no guards.

Luxembourg got off rather easily in the War. The Germans occupied it at the outset. I was put right on one thing by the Nafzigers. I had supposed that the German army marched in rough-shod over the Luxembourgers. There was the story of the Grand Duchess meeting the Germans on a bridge and forbidding them to cross. I was told that was a joke. She met them. She may have entered a technical protest. But actually it was in the nature of a welcome. She was so well known for pro-Germanism that after the war she had to resign and her place was taken by her younger sister, Charlotte, who is now in power and is popular.

Before the War, the Duchy of Luxembourg belonged to the German customs union. I suppose Germany expected to absorb Luxembourg in due course. Doubtless, she would have done so if she had succeeded in the War. That is the way things go— in Germanic countries, not in British countries. I am told that throughout the War the Germans in Luxembourg acted fairly decently—for Germans. They paid for what they got and the prices were good. But at that the Luxembourgers got thoroughly fed up. The occupation cured them of any possibility of Nazism. There are a few Nazis in Luxembourg but they came from Germany.

I spoke of these things to a variety of people in Luxembourg and there was no difference of opinion amongst them—not even as to the policy of Luxembourg in relation to Germany. They have their own domestic politics. There are liberals and conservatives, and the Church is a factor. They even have their opinions on German politics—for the Germans, some, as I learn of Mr. Nafziger, Senior (he was born in Germany) have a tenderness for Hitler and think he is a good thing for Germany. But though those in the eastern part of the Duchy are almost pure German they want nothing to do with Germany as a political or national force.

One of my conversations was with the barber to whom I went twice, so that was an old customer. You know how barbers talk. He was free in his expression. He thought the Germans were verrückt (i.e. crazy, off their base). He said his father used to say the Germans had a crazy streak in them. They were crazy before the War and crazy after it. A German paper was being delivered through the street, apparently a religious paper. It featured a statement by the Pope, just made, to the effect that he had seen the first Reich with Bismarck rise and fall; then he has seen another rise and fall; and now he was seeing the third in ascendancy. That is good stuff for a Luxembourg religious paper. It was someone here who called my attention to the fact that the Pope had left Rome to avoid the humiliation of not having Hitler call on him. No, I think Hitler has thoroughly estranged the Roman Catholic Church. And one of the consequences is a feeling of rapprochement between the Roman Catholic people and

Protestants—not necessarily the Roman Catholic clergy, though the
Protestant clergy have a much more kindly feeling toward the Roman
Catholic Church on account of the persecution in Germany.

Irrel, Rhineland-Palatinate, Germany.[20] May 11, 1938

As soon as you cross the border from Luxembourg into Germany
you find: women working in the fields; oxen, i.e. cows, for transport
and draft; blonds; hard-working faces; more <u>mist</u> in the villages;
soldiers; trenches; fortifications; officers; ditto driving like h———;
peasants working late into the night; German kolossal architecture;
head-kerchiefs.

Schuld,[21] Rhineland-Palatinate. May 11, 1938

Yesterday afternoon, crossing the border at Echternach with a
minimum of difficulty, I took my way to Bitburg. Near the town, at
Lessen, was the birthplace of the Nafzigers senior.... The old farm
was in the hands of a Peter Nafziger, a nephew of the three old
gentlemen of who I have spoken. Mina seemed to think I ought to
drop in there for a snapshot or two for the uncle in America.

    Peter is a Nazi. He started with the usual line of what did one
think of Germany in the Ausland.[22] I told him some. He came right
back with the Jewish press theory. It was the Jews that poisoned
public opinion in other countries against Germany. I suppose it is
natural enough, but what can you do with such people? The Jews,
according to Peter, were the authors of the Versailles treaty, which
oppressed the poor Germans so. It never occurs to these people
that they deserved any punishment for starting the War. And the rest
of the world is too decent to remind them of it. How could I tell Peter
that they were getting only part of what was coming to them? ...
Even the Mennonites are satisfied with things as they are. The loss
of a bit of liberty is nothing in their young lives. Oh, yes, another
thing—didn't I think the Jews were the cause of unemployment in
the United States and in England in spite of the fact that there was
so much gold in these countries? It might have been worthwhile
to demonstrate to Peter that the cause of unemployment was high
wages, and that Germany was wise or lucky enough to have escaped
that evil. But Peter was intelligent. He was up on his Nazi politics.
How they get away with it intellectually as Mennonites is a puzzle
to me. But, of course, there was going to be no war. The Fuehrer
would get the colonies and everything without any war. This much

I will grant Peter, that Hitlerism was a defense against communism. It doesn't occur to them that the two are of the same stripes— politically, not economically.

A little later on May 11, 1938
A fellow has just come along and delivered the morning paper through the window with a "Heil Hitler" to me, to which I replied with an emphatic "Guten Morgen."[23] The hotel man, sitting on the other side of the room smiled. After a pause I said to him: "That can one still undertake?" He laughed and said "Sicherlich" (surely); "an outlander can that do." And there was a suggestion in his tone as if he would liked to have added "you know damn well I wouldn't 'Heil' if I didn't have to."

A yoke of oxen just trudged by.

All the same it seems to me that in some cases the "Heil Hitler" comes out with a snarl. Of course I suppose these Germans cultivate a hide that can bear this sort of thing. For one of us it would be a terrible humiliation to go through this "Heil Hitler." I think perhaps the main consideration is that we are different. These people were lick-spittling in the time of the Kaiser, and they have cultivated no particular inhibitions since. And in another five or ten years they may heil someone or something else.

Almost everywhere, so far, in Europe, including, I think, though I am not quite sure, Italy, the farmers have been taking mangle wurtzels out of pits for their cattle. These pits seem generally to be beside the road, perhaps for convenience of access, though for that I don't see why beside the lane would not do as well. These mangles, I am told, are fed to eke out the pasture in its early stages. I saw chickens eating the mangles when they had plenty of grass. From what I have seen in Luxembourg and Germany, the single-comb brown Leghorn seems to be the favourite. I have seen no Barred Plymouth Rocks. I haven't seen a poultry farm.[24]

In the Ahr Valley, near Ahrweiler, Rhineland-Palatinate. Later still May 11, 1938
This is so beautiful that it hurts. It is more <u>humanly</u> beautiful than the French Riviera. But there is even a little palm in the garden to my right. I have stopped in the street to try to take in the pleasure of it—the warm sunshine, the pear and apple blossoms, the songs of the birds, strange yet familiar, the nice looking people, the

particularly nice-looking girls—blond for the most part, but possible for any drawing room though they may be of peasant class. A peasant here seems to be under no disadvantage as such. He (or she) is capable of anything.

Cologne, also on May 11, 1983

This is not on my way to Bad Nauheim but I wanted to see the Cathedral, and it was only a little way up from Bonn, which was on my way. It was worthwhile coming here to see a cathedral with its towers finished. I wonder if it is because it is German....

Later—It is pretty hard to say anything without revealing one's ignorance. Now I find that in 1842 the foundation stone was laid for the completion of Cologne Cathedral. So it was incomplete until that time, and does not, therefore, stand as a monument to German thoroughness before that time.

But however (as the French would say) is Cologne really a German cathedral? It is on the left bank of the Rhine, and the French for hundreds of years contended for the Rhine as the boundary throughout. And under Napoleon was not their claim effectuated? The valleys of the Saar and the Moselle, which flow into the Rhine from the west could be French—as they were of old Roman. And, of course they were, after the late War, given a chance to be French. I wonder whether there was really a secret ballot or whether it was something like the vote for the Anschluss with Austria.

[The cathedral is] as beautiful and satisfactory inside as outside: and it is clean. The only sound I heard in the interior was that of a vacuum cleaner. Really, no comment by way of comparing the Germans with the French on the score of cleanliness could be more explicit than a true comparison between this church and, for example, Chartres or Notre Dame.

But somebody has something to say about the fact that the cathedrals are finished in Germany and not in France. And it is not to the credit of the Germans.... There are no churches in Germany worth seeing except those along the western edge, like Cologne. Civilization and Christianity found their way really among the Gauls but the German tribes resisted both—as they do now.

At the turn of the first 1000 years there was were still many heathens in the German hinterlands. And during the twelfth and thirteenth centuries when church architecture flourished in France and England and the German peoples were for the most part still *too primitive and rude to attempt any large enterprise—except by way of fighting.*

All this notwithstanding that the Romans had penetrated far into Germany and subdued it in part and for a time. Roman ruins such as those near Bitburg show that Romans lived in luxury in parts of Germany, no doubt utilizing the natives as slaves. But the natives did not, apparently, as did the Gauls of England and France, take to Roman culture and incorporate it as their own.

Has it come back to constructing a Hadrian's Wall to keep out the barbarians—a Chinese wall to protect civilization form the Mongols? That is what the Maginot Line really is.

Bad Nauheim, Baden-Württemberg. May 13, 1938

[Wegenast arrived here late on May 11.] The Kercknoff Foundation, as it is called is a magnificent affair and is, I believe, the best, if indeed not the only, institution of its kind in the world, being devoted entirely to diseases of the heart. It is purely a research institution and does not treat patients unless incidentally to research. Working as it does in conjunction with the State authorities who manage the enormous therapeutic bathing establishment, it is in a position to do work which would be impossible anywhere else. The number of patients per year in Bad Nauheim is about 30,000. Before the War it was 45,000.

I had made some inquires of the head porter of the hotel on the basis of which I asked for the secretary of the institute. Through an English-speaking lady in the secretary's office I was put in touch with Herr Doctor Koch who seemed to be in some kind of executive position besides doing scientific work. He spoke English quite well. I said I had come to consult with someone in Bad Nauheim about certain important questions which I had laid out in a memorandum I had brought with me.[25] I wanted to have the services of a man who would go over the memorandum and advise me for a proper fee. He said they were concerned in his institution only with theoretical work and they did not take patients, but he wanted to know what the problems were. I gave him my memorandum. He quickly got the high spots of the memorandum and congratulated me on my scientific approach. I congratulated him on his lawyerlike grasp. He said he was not competent to deal with the matter himself as his line was physics; but he would put me in touch with the proper man.

The plant for treating patients to the various baths is of course elaborate and extensive. [It] involved an expenditure of millions of dollars, and it speaks strongly against any probability that amongst so practical a people as the Germans it could be ... a hoax or anything less than a scientifically sound undertaking. That in itself practically settled one of my questions. That question was whether, in view of the fact that baths for heart disease were practically unknown in medical practice in America, the German and other European physicians who prescribed baths were either fools or knaves.

Bad Nauheim. May 15, 1938

Met Dr. Wachter by appointment this morning, to discuss my memorandum. He is a very positive man. I suppose that has its uses from the standpoint of applied therapeutics. It is not the mark of a scientist. Dr. Wachter says the CO_2 is the important element in the Nauheim waters. The salts are not so important.... From the medical standpoint the sum total of my visit to Bad Nauheim seems to be:

1) Baths with water containing CO_2 are indicated in certain heart cases;
2) They must be applied with care and skill based on intensive experience, lest they do harm;
3) The exact reactions of the baths are not fully known;
4) CO_2 may be absorbed into the system through the skin.

I am afraid that, as in the case of most, if not all, medical practice, there is a certain amount of applied psychology practiced along with therapeutics proper. No doubt the patient's faith in the remedy has in some cases and in some degree an influence on its remedial effect. But that does not seem to be the whole story. It is well known, or at all events well believed, that only certain waters are efficacious for heart affections and the common factor is the presence of CO_2. That goes as between the various countries of Europe, each of which would be only too glad to have the heart patients as tourists if the proper water was available. But the water is to be found principally in Bad Nauheim in Germany and at Royat in France. So there is where you find concentrated the business of trying to cure heart disease by bathing.

All this indicates a certain suspicion of doubt. And this doubt is exploited if not indeed propagated, by the medical profession in America, whose members seem quite prepared to let their patients suspect the medical profession in Europe. We are allowed to believe that the practice of medicine in Europe is more "commercialized"

*etc. than in God's country. The worst that can be said for them is
that, beginning with the empirical fact that people thought they
felt better after taking the baths, they sought to find why this was
so. It is nothing against the doctors at Nauheim that they cannot
answer all the whys. They are resolving one after another by patient
research. They do not know as yet how the carbon dioxide operated
upon the arteries and capillaries to make them relax. They think it
may be some relation by electricity between the ions of the CO_2 and
the cells of the blood vessels. They do know, they tell me, that some
of the CO_2 is used up and they do know that the blood vessels relax
and the blood pressure decreases.[26]*

*Toward the close of the afternoon I sat down in the Tennis Café
for a cup of tea. It was quite an experience. Everything here is an
experience. I see so many things reminiscent of the old days at
Waterloo, Ontario.*

Bad Nauheim. May 22, 1938

*Things look bad in Czecho-Slovakia.[27] Is Hitler going to make another
coup? The "Times" was not distributed until late this afternoon—
some person or persons no doubt waiting to have their minds
made up whether to let it go for circulation. People in the rest of
the world will be very nervous. I can't bring myself to believe that
these Germans are going to fight; not now. Dr. Wachter said, "for
two or three million Sudeten Germans we are not going into war."
I am confident that he expresses the feeling of the great mass
of business and professional people in Germany. These people
absolutely do not want war. For one thing, they expect Hitler to get
them everything they want by peaceful means. They want <u>peace</u>. I
think it would cost Hitler his job and his life immediately if he were to
plunge Germany into war. The rest of the world does not understand
Hitler's position as it is understood here. He is the* Fuehrer *(leader)
of the German people—not their boss. He does what the people
want. He <u>leads</u> them where they want to go. He takes his cue from
the bulk of the business and professional people and he makes
it his business to be completely advised. There is a good deal of
substance in the contention sometimes made by Germans that their
government is really democratic. Of course that is not the whole
story. But this much is clear: for the policies of Germany you must
hold the German people responsible. Hitler is only one of them.*

Tennis Café, Bad Nauheim. May 28, 1938

Opposite me at this little table for four is a Heinie—a real one. He is reading a newspaper as I write. If he knew what I was writing he would <u>bust</u>. He is square-head, blond, baldish, tall, adipose, middle-aged, wears a swastika in his button hole. This fellow was certainly in the War. He would be a Kaiser fan. Now he is one of the regulars, a perfect Hitler fan—probably a member of the <u>party</u>, getting reasonably good pickings.

Although there are nothing but Heinies, male and female, around—and thick as flies, one does not feel over-borne. They are so keen to have Ausländer here, and particularly Engländer, that you can sort of kick them in the shins (or somewhere else if you like) and they just take it and pretend they like it. All this sort of goes on mentally and implicitly though not a sign is made.

These birds do not want to fight England again.

Actually, Journal, I am having the time of my life right now, sizing these guys up—and their women. This crowd is so typical, so <u>average</u> of reasonably well-to-do commercial and professional people. Lots of them are nice—quite O.K. Some may be all right in spite of their square heads. (Of course they haven't nearly all square heads—not half.) But there is a fellow over there, who may be a doctor or a banker, with a heart condition perhaps. He has the darndest head. It pyramids from all four side and comes to a point.

My friend opposite has got up and asked me politely if I will please tell the waiter that he has left a mark lying on his tray for his tea. He is in a hurry. When he smiles he is just like a human being. I wouldn't mind doing business with him. He just as a matter of course treated me as an equal. I can't work up any more steam against him. That is one of the difficulties here. There are so many of them that turn out to be decent—really recent. You get all thrown out of your stride. Now there have come to the table two young couples just as nice as you could wish. They might be any two nice couples in Toronto or Ottawa.

Just tumbled to something. I <u>thought</u> there was something strange about the looks of many of the boys between ten and sixteen years of age—and the girls too of the same age, with braids hanging down their backs or their fronts. At this age they go around here bare headed. I thought they looked somehow unusual apart from their unusual blondness. Now I have what is wrong. <u>They have square</u>

heads, both the boys and the girls (it seems more terrible in a girl). When they are older and have hats on you don't notice it.

What a pity: They are nice clean healthy-looking animals. But if the Hitler philosophy is to prevail there is no place for them or their progeny in our world. I say our world—the world of culture, the world of gentle men and women. For if the German theory is to prevail it is a war of extinction between two political philosophies. The German theory of course is that the German idea is to prevail über alles. Well, if it is to be fought out on the basis of force it has still to be demonstrated that force alone must necessarily prevail over force plus reason plus gentleness. Force did not prevail in 1914. But this sort of thing must surely come to an end sometime. We thought we had ended it in 1918. If we should win the next time must we get maudlin again and let them off? Hitler's policy as expressed in his original "Mein Kampf" (the publication [of the original version] which is now suppressed) was that France was to be exterminated— vernichet.[28] If that is the policy of the German people, is there anything for the French to do but meet it with a similar policy, or can we still hope for the leopard to change his spots? And it is from this stock, according to the German theory, that a race of supermen is to be bred. This whole race business must be known to the Germans themselves to be crazy. If it is a matter of Nordics and blonds, the Danes and Norwegians and Swedes and Finns and Czechs and Magyars ought to be peopling the earth. Denmark has not room for her people. Why should she not demand colonies? Why should she not drang nach osten?[29] But these people have no logic—only sentiment. They get some crazy theory—almost any one will do what pleases their vanity—and then they ride it to the most illogical conclusions.... The proper eugenic policy in Germany would be to prevent square-heads from breeding or intermarrying with the rest of the population. Where did these square-heads come from anyway? Is it a Mongol or a Tartar strain? That will have to be looked into. I wonder if Darwin has anything about it....

The other day, at Bad Nauheim, I bought me a copy of Rosenberg's "Mythus des 20ten Jahrhunderts."[30] This is the Nazi bible. In the book shops it is displayed as prominently as [the latest version of] "Mein Kampf." Rosenberg is the intellectual Moses (or perhaps Aaron) of the present German wonderings.[31] But it is such another case as that of Marx. He is going to give the German people, and through them the world at large, a new historical assessment.

*And you may take it to be a sort of Anglo-Saxon understatement.
Hear what the gentleman has to say for himself in the first few
sentences of his book.*

> *Today there begins one of those epochs in which the history of
> the world must be written anew. The old pictures of humanity's
> past have faded out; the outlines of the acting personalities
> now reveal themselves as mis-drawn, their motivation falsely
> indicated, their whole being for the most part entirely misjudged.
> A sense of life, young, yet consciously primeval, presses to
> take form; a world conception is born, and, strong-willed,
> makes its beginning, with old forms, sanctified usages and
> inherited capacity to analyze itself. No longer historically, but
> fundamentally. Not in special domains, but everywhere. Not only
> in the twigs, but also in the roots.*

*(Note the way, that he thinks the Germans are capable of analyzing
themselves!) Brave words these. But they bode no good for logic
or common sense. Rather, they forebode storm, emotion, [and]
unreason. But listen to the next paragraph.*

> *And the sign of our time is: renunciation of the unlimited
> absolute, i.e. assertion by* one *for himself, of an individual
> relationship to everything in the way of experience and
> communal value, in order to bring about, either peacefully
> or forcibly, a superhuman community of souls of* all. *The
> "Christianization of the world" was at one time such a goal; and
> its salvation by a second-coming Christ. As another objective
> there was propounded the "humanization of mankind." Both
> ideals were buried in the bloody chaos and in the new birth
> of the experience of the world-war, notwithstanding that, right
> now, both the one and the other are acquiring constantly more
> fanaticizing priesthood and following. These are benumbing
> processes; not vivifying life—a belief which died in the soul
> cannot be revived from the dead.*[32]

*What a whopper for a premise! Anyone who will swallow that need
not gag at a little sour logic. Let us look into it a bit.*
*Do you sense the bitterness of it? Think of the gulf between
the sentiments displayed [by Rosenberg] and the real (though not*

unmixed) desire of the rest of the world to make the world (including Germany) safe for democracy and Christianity and humanity and decency.... Rosenberg [states] that the attempt to Christianize and humanize mankind was a disastrous mistake, [and] has been wiped out by the War. The idea of improving the world by those methods is [now] dead. That is what he thinks. He is ready to give the Germans the real dope. Of course the farthest from his mind is that the Germans may have been to blame for bringing on the War. By their sabotaging of all the previous efforts to attain general disarmament—their attitude toward the Hague Convention, the Parliament of parliaments and all other movements to banish war. And then by invading Belgium and sinking the Lusitania, and introducing poison gas, and bombing civilian populations.

No; the thing is, says Rosenberg, not to be less German but to be more German. Get rid of the impurities in the German blood. That's it. Blood is the thing—blood and iron. Strength—strength through (not for) joy. Strength at any cost. Nerves of steel—not to give way as they did in the last war. Be tough. Train yourself from infancy to be a tough guy. Christianity?! A meek and lowly Jew, with his sermon on the Mount? Phooey!

May we make one or two further observations on these two first short paragraphs? Obviously he is appealing to the Germans' sense of having lost something in the War. And he undertakes to tell them what it was that was "buried in the bloody chaos and in the new birth" of the war. He says it was the idea that Christiani[ty was] humanizing the world [that was buried]. The rest of the world had thought, had hoped, that it was the German will to fight that was buried—the thing that had kept the world on tenterhooks for the past hundred years. But no, says Rosenberg, we mustn't lose that. It is the only thing worth living for. Be yourself. Be German. Are the lines drawn clearly enough? Can there be any compromise between Christianity and humanity on the one hand and this thing on the other? Rosenberg does not intend that there shall be. And he wants us to know in the first page of his book that they are going places, "not in special domains, but everywhere." That, indeed, is more important than whether they know where they are going or whether they ought to go at all.... And did you note that it is to be "either peacefully or forcibly"?

And so he proceeds to lay down his philosophy of race.... Why race? Why not morality? Why not Sittlichkeit?[33] Why not the idea of gentleness—of being a gentleman—for which there is no word in the German language. Why race? Because he sees his way to whipping his people into unreasoning emotion about their being Deutsch. And so he starts his Nordics (or pure Aryans that compose the master race) off from the continent of Atlantis, of which, only Greenland remains. He spreads [Aryans] across the north of Africa (hence the blue-eyed Berbers) into Libya, where they constitute the pre-dynastic ruling class. [Aryans] go on to India, where they invent the caste system to preserve their race purity as Brahmins. They turn up as "Amorites" in Palestine and founded Jerusalem; and a "layer" of these are found in Galilee "where Jesus was to emerge"—Just like that—he doesn't say Jesus was Nordic—but you can do some thinking for yourself.

Oh yes, of course the ancient Greeks were [Aryans] too and the Latins—and the Macedonians. (It wouldn't do to leave out Alexander.) The Persians, naturally, and even the Sumerians—in short wherever there were good fighters and a worthwhile "Kultur"... He doesn't even leave out the Scotch! He says there are traces there of [Aryans] from the Stone age. Have a heart, dear Reader, and let me know your reaction to that.... Talk about re-writing history! ... A new history! In which the Germans are to be the authors of everything worthwhile in the ancient or modern world—the culture of Egypt, of Assyria, of Greece, of Rome, of Mexico even. Tacitus and Caesar of course are entirely wrong in their descriptions of these barbarians. The forts which the cultured Romans built to keep back the savage tribes—what a dreadful mistake. The Germans should have been welcomed for the purity of their blood-stream. About that blood stream—how does it come that lying historians were permitted to spread the story that Asiatic hordes from time to time swept in across the steppes—Tartars, Mongols, Huns. The marshes which came to be the site of the most parvenu of world-cities, Berlin, and which still exude their miasmas at night—once the site of a Tartar encampment. There was then no Rosenberg to guarantee purity of blood for the offspring of German maidens. What is the Prussian square-head but a by-product of the Tartar invasions? ... The mingling with hostile blood brings the end of civilization, says Rosenberg, "and in this blood-prostitution there die personality, people, race, civilization."... The text is in places obscure and hard to translate;[34] but there are certain clear meanings: It is the race *and not the individual that counts. It is blood that tells. There is a sub-conscious blood-relationship and blood-law which the individual should obey rather than his own untrained reason and his own bent. If he doesn't it will be just too bad—for himself or somebody—or something. And if you mix blood it will be just too bad too. And if you are not conscious of the shamefulness of thus betraying your blood that is because you had not had sufficient intellectual training to bring out, or replace, the sub-conscious blood-verities.*

Heidelberg, Baden-Württemberg, Germany. May 30, 1938

I finally got away from Bad Nauheim. I was bound to get away (of which more anon) but it gave me a pang to leave Frau Siedle and Mia, the chamber-maid, who had been so faithful and decent while I was confined to my room.

I had written to Sofie Wegenast at Heidelberg, sister of Carl, of Trieste, in response to a note from her, asking me to come to see them. I suggested a flexible appointment for her and her sister Emma to have dinner at the hotel with me tonight subject to the exigencies of health, travel, etc. When I got here I found that Fräulein Wegenast had telephoniert asking to be told when I arrived; and presently it was arranged through the porter that the two of them would come down. I am waiting for them now.

Heidelberg. May 31, 1938

We had a very interesting evening—relatives from far asunder meeting for the first time in several generations. We talked of this and that, and presently came the inevitable question of what one thought of Germany.... I let them down easily. Only a few odd touches like telling them that to most people in my country I should hardly admit that I had gone to Germany. That was a bit of a poser but it did not hold [them] for very long. They ... expatiated on the marvels of Hitlerism and on the wicked Jewish press ... which spread such false news and opinions about Germany. When I told them about Tel-Aviv (which ought to have been a relief to them but somehow isn't) Emma told me that the Jews were coming back to Germany.[35] They were dissatisfied in Palestine and other countries and are coming back. I said, "You astonish me. How could they come back here?" She said, with a little toss of her head, "Oh, well, we don't mind having a certain number, a certain percentage, but they must not get frech; if they do they will get what is coming to them." Now Emma is a bright girl. She was in some sort of executive position—I have no doubt a good one. Indeed I have really no business to speak familiarly of her as a girl. She was a young woman of considerable attainments. She was the kind of young woman who thought as men thought. What she said would be the kind of thing men would say. And what she said about the Jews she was no doubt expressing the general informed business man's view. Therein, I think, lies the significance of what she said. There may have been a bit of feminine malice in the prompt attempt to depreciate the Jewish success in Tel-Aviv; but when she said they were prepared to have a certain percentage of Jews in Germany I think she was not expressing an original idea of her own or one opposed to general opinion. Emma also wanted to know why Canada did not separate herself from England. There was a certain malice (in the French sense) in the question but I replied that of course the one thing one wanted was to be British—that Canada and the other Dominions were free to do as they please but preferred to remain English. She knew well enough how the land lay.

Shall we philosophize a moment about the use of the word "Heinies"? I was just going to write "Germans," when it seemed inadequate. Why did I choose the other word? It implies of course a certain contemptuous familiarity. But that is not all. It implies a pity that verges on tenderness. The poor devils! They don't know what it is all about. And they sense this attitude on our part. Hence the chip-on-the-shoulder attitude. Hence the anxiety to know what we think of them. Hence the inferiority complex.

By the way, Reader, have you thought of the difference in attitude between calling the German a Heinie and calling the Frenchman a Frog? There's one for you to work out.

Oh, quite, quite—You may not have that attitude. But the great throng of Americans—Canadian and United Statesan—and Englishmen also—think "Frog" and "Heinie" and "Kike" and "Wop." And that means something; don't kid yourself.

Plankstadt, Baden-Württemberg. May 31, 1938

Meet Master Hans Müller of Friederichstrasse 44, Plankstadt, Baden, Germany. He is the central figure in this snapshot.[36] I had stopped in his village to get something out of the back of the car. As usual a flock of youngsters immediately gathered round to see the *strange big car and to hear the radio, Hans amongst them. I asked Hans to lift the lid of the back of the car for me, and for that I took a photo of him and promised to send it. Hans is a nice lad. He will make a good, loyal Nazi and he is not a square-head.*

How nice and clean and well-dressed the kids are. It is that way everywhere I have been in Germany. They are certainly as well-dressed and as well-kept as any corresponding lot of village children in America.

In his research into Mennonite history, he talked to a number of Germans about Hitler. Richard Lichti and his wife had Wegenast stay with them—they were very kind.

Hochspeyer, Rhineland-Palatinate, Germany. June 1, 1938
Richard Lichti had kept me up until after midnight talking Nazism. As a guest I couldn't very well disagree with him.... Now I must finish my story about the Lichtis—at least what I have time to tell; for they were extraordinarily kind that I must wear out the patience of the dear reader by trying to tell it all.

I left Richard Litchi with considerable regret although it was hard to put up with his enthusiastic Hitlerism. Feelings get pretty well mixed up under such circumstances. There is no question in my mind of the whole-hearted friendship of the whole family toward me, even though they know that politically I am from their standpoint a total loss.

Richard holds several quasi-judicial offices of which he is very proud. He showed me his "Heil Hitler" letters announcing his appointments. One office is that of "Ortsbauernfuhrer." (The great thing in Germany is to be a Fuhrer of some kind.) That is to say, he is one of a local court of three judges who have to decide in the case of a farmer who has died without a will, which of the children is to have the old farm and how much he is to pay the other children. The policy of the government is not to break up the old farmsteads into fractional pieces, to give the choice of the place, first to the youngest son, if he is competent, and if he declines them to the next youngest, and so on up. Then a valuation is placed on the farm and the son who takes it has to pay off the other children in periodical payments.·

Then Richard is also a member of another court which has authority to step in where a farm is not being properly managed. They may give the owner another chance, or they may make him step out and put someone else in, who must undertake to pay the owner at a valuation fixed by the court.

Richard would just as soon have the world know that he is by way of being somebody....

Oh yes, here are a few notes I made around Richard's gardens: No fruit this year—everything frozen—hard frost—even snow. Snowballs and peonies. Same grass and weeds we have in Ontario. Catnip, Nettles, Cheese-weed (mallow), Plantain a little different— reddish. English plantain here too—a little larger. Habit of growth of trees—e.g. Plum, cherry etc., same as in Ontario—not like in England. Buttercups.

These Nazis are clever. They put themselves out to cultivate class consciousness and then they lead and direct it. Look at this card which Richard gave me: It plays on the theme, "Lo the poor farmer, he gets it in the neck every time." Then they give it a turn that he is doing his stuff for Deutschland, and that makes everything o.k. Shall I translate the chorus: "We do not fight for ourselves alone, we guard the rights of our forefathers. We want to be servants of our people, we Germans of German race." (Query: what rights of any forefathers are being guarded; and who is threatening them?)

Wissembourg, Alsace, France. June 3, 1938

Out of Germany again. Whew! What a relief. I dare say it is a matter of psychology and disposition, but to me Germany is a charnel house. Liberty is dead and rotting. The Germans not only do not care but they do not understand. Even if he intellectually understands the workings of Magna Carta and the Habeas Corpus Act the German doesn't see anything desirable about having things that way. It doesn't worry him to have Niemoeller and Schuschnigg held without trial. They must deserve it or they wouldn't be held. And they are ready with arguments as to why they should not be at liberty. What can you do with people like that? If they read this they would not see in it any condemnation.

Almost the first thing the French Customs officials put to me, interrogatively, that it was beau "over there." They are pleased and relieved at my prompt response that it was a great relief to be again in a free country.

The landlady here, at the Hotel des Angles (formerly zum Engel), at an early stage put the same question and was expansively

*[happy] at my reply. "Sure" she understood. She spoke French to
me but German to the servants—and afterwards broke familiarly
into German with me. But* they know and understand *how dumb the
Germans are. And yet they watch anxiously the rapid progress of the
German people in the art of living.*

*It seems as if the French were cussedly avoiding work and
refusing it because they do not want to be like the Germans.*

Wissembourg, Alsace. June 4, 1938

*This is France all right. After getting up at 10 o'clock (stayed in bed
to celebrate being out of Germany) and having a breakfast of rolls
(white once more) honey and hot milk, I sallied forth to get a cheque
cashed. No luck. All banks closed,* because it is Saturday. *This is the
land of the forty hour week, where it is a crime to work on Saturday.
I finally did find a money-changer, and a very decent one who
supplied me with French money at the proper rate.*

*You don't get very far in France before you get impatient with
the labour situation. The people themselves, outside the rabid
labour fans, are getting fed up. The 40-hour week is a serious joke
to mention of which will always get a rise out of any business man
or farmer. Everyone expects a change, but nobody is doing anything
about it—except the government, which is now hedging away from
it by decrees permitting exceptions. It is a curious situation which
seems to defy any effort at logical explanation.*

*In the days of their misery, at the time of the Revolution and for
some time after, the French people collectively and individually
exhibited a capacity for unselfishness amounting to fanaticism.
Fraternité means more in French that it does to an Englishman.
Family relationship and feeling are notorious for solidarity among
Latins. And to extend fraternité to one's fellow citizens had more
meaning to them than has any brand of socialism today. They
still have Liberté, Egalité, Fraternité on their coins, but in practice
it is pretty much dog eat dog. French politics and public life are
unequalled for corruption. And nobody is doing anything about
it. The French elections are not won by showing the other side is
corrupt. So a benevolent autocracy to a Frenchman is nothing more
than a contradiction in terms. The Frenchman believes in equality of
opportunity to get at the public trough. The idea of having the same*

government in power for ten, twenty, thirty years, as we have seen it in Canada, would be terrifying to a Frenchman. The members of government would have made all the money in the world long before such a period could elapse.

But I should not have started philosophizing yet. As usual I am behind in my story. (One couldn't very well be ahead?) There are the events of yesterday in Germany to recount before I forget them— especially my visit to the Herr Doktor Neff.

I found my way as quickly as I could from Frankfurt to Kirchheim-Bolanden. At Oppenheim I had to cross the Rhine, not on a bridge but on a boat which was warped sideways from one side of the river to the other by a cable arrangement. While waiting for the boat I had the radio going and through it got into a conversation with a truck driver and a soldier. The soldier was getting a ride with the truck to Wörrstadt, where he lived. When he knew I was going through Wörrstadt he readily accepted my invitation to ride with me. He put his pack in the back of the car and we drove off. We had quite a talk. He did most of the talking. He had been in the army for nine years and had now been given, by way of promotion, a position as gendarme at Wörrstadt. He was full of enthusiasm, which he expected me to share, for the things Hitler was doing. Large factories were being erected all over Germany and production was going ahead. They were learning to do without the things from other countries. They were making gasoline from coal and cloth from wood.

I went over to Weierhof to see Dr. Neff. The Herr Doktor was indeed remarkably well informed [about Mennonite history] on every point I touched in my inquiries. There is really very little excuse for the ignorance of American Mennonites as to their origin and history—at all the events for four hundred years back. I would be prepared to overlook, and even justify, the hooks and eyes and other items of old fashion, but I do not see how the prevailing ignorance can be justified. I know, and in part appreciate the indisposition of the Amish toward higher education, but surely they ought to know why they are the way they are—and how. But that means a knowledge of their history at least as far back as the year 1525, when the Mennonite or Anabaptist or Wiedertaufer or Taufgesinnten element separated out from those who chose to stand by Zwingle in his project of uniting the church and the state.

Wissenbourg, France. June 4th, 1938

Now I must try to set in order some of the observations which I have been in a position to make during the last few weeks, but which, for obvious reasons I have hesitated to put in writing or, above all things, to commit to the mail. With one thing and another, over a period of several weeks of stay in Germany I have come to some definite opinions as to the lay of the land. I may not always give details of particular conversations with particular individuals. One learns to avoid that. Not that one goes about with bated breath exactly. I found it possible to talk quite freely. Anyone who is not building for a future (or a present) in Germany may talk over the affairs and the policies of the day pretty freely. After all they can't put everybody in gaol. And there is not so much "hush hush" as you might think. Indeed you might say that politics is the one thing they want to talk about to an Ausländer. I may also say things that contradict one another. It is not so easy to generalize about 75,000,000 people.

The ordinary commerce of life in Germany is no more strictly supervised by the police as far as I can see, than is the case in any other country. The people themselves are no doubt more orderly than some others—the Irish for example. But it is not by way of compulsion. I disobeyed the parking regulations in Bad Nauheim both unwittingly and wittingly and there was never a word said. In the cities the passers-by are quick and decent to tell you when you are going the wrong way on a one-way street: but in Köln the other day I kept right on going to the next street and nothing happened. It was right beside the Cathedral. They are so glad to have tourists that they would let them do almost anything.

If you adopt a superior supercilious attitude towards things German, and, in particular, political, they take it lying down. Either they agree or they expect it as a matter of course. I don't know why. They are no less friendly. And it is not obsequiousness—unless they are so practiced that they avoid showing their feelings—but I don't think so. The Germans were getting along well enough before the advent of Hitler. The tremendous progress of Germany since the War was not all made in the last five years. The most important items were made before that. It is because Germany was getting on her feet that Nazism arose. It is there for anyone to see, though the Germans themselves are least ready to see: but the factories, the houses, the roads were largely built before Hitlerism got into its stride. I have in mind one village which I had known seventeen years ago. When I saw it this time it was improved out of all recognition—new and better houses, streets, etc. But those improvements were at least five years old. It is utterly and profoundly correct to distinguish between Germans as individuals and the Germans as an aggregate entity. Even a small group of Germans is less desirable than an individual or individuals. As they exercise their organizing faculty they seem to exude or precipitate something that makes them objectionable.

The Germans can analyze anything else but themselves. Not that they are always correct. But they try. And how? But it is on themselves that they do the worst job. They get maudlin and sorry for themselves.

The German is a man of adjectives. The Englishman avoids them. It has not occurred to the German that there is anything offensive or lowering about the use of adjectives. The Englishman goes part of the way with the Japanese in depreciating and depreciating everything that is his.... His house, his horse, his dog—even his wife, are nothing to brag about or enthuse over—not to other people. But need I tell you, there may be some slight difference between what he says and what he thinks?

But to the German things are wunderbar—not only that but woo-oo-oounderbah-AHrr. The German orator smacks his lips over every adjective and most adverbs and makes everyone the occasion of a vocal display. To the Englishman this is simply putrid—the height of ill-breeding and undesirability. The very qualities which the Germans most lack they are now prevented from cultivating. Discernment, political disquisition, recognition of chicanery, grim humour, any kind of humour involving political bearings, are all too dangerous to be indulged in. One oblique word might wreck a career. One unguarded allusion could destroy a reputation which otherwise might lead to membership in the "party," the highest honour (?) not attainable by a German in the ordinary course, unless in a military way.

Democracy may by the same token be an oligarchy of politicians. But politicians do not agree. It is their business not to agree. And when they fall out the honest (?) voter may just possibly get his due—if he is smart enough. And it is a part of the business of a democratic government (not necessarily of this or that politician) to see that the voter gets smart. That is the system. Well in Germany the businessmen leave getting the votes in the capable hands of Adolf Hitler. Then it is simply a matter of getting together and deciding what is best for the country, the party, business, or whatever you like to think. And it is the business of these men to agree. They consist of people who were smart enough to jump on the Hitler bandwagon soon enough, and also a few, who were so smart that they didn't need to jump on the band wagon.

The business of an individual under such a system is not to have opinions but to stand in with the government and get what he can for himself. The price he pays for what he gets is the greatest measure of loyalty, not to his country or his people or their interests, but to the person or persons immediately above him in the governmental hierarchy.

The Germans always were adept sycophants. They are steeped in respect for authority. They had centuries of training and practice under their local princelings. The English cockney heckler would be an ununderstandable phenomenon to them.

At present certain individuals enjoy certain very definite social, financial and other advantages by virtue of the favour of the Party. They are placed at the head of industries and other undertakings. They can get money from banks when other people cannot. They drive around Germany in large, high-powered cars. They are obviously well fed and well massaged and well tailored. And many of them seem pretty well leisured—although it is the fashion in Germany to appear to be busy at something, even if it is only riding automobiles. The proprietor of the hotel at Bad Nauheim is an example. He spends most of his time, apparently, driving in his big Mercedes-Benz to Frankfurt, Wiesbaden, Heidelberg, etc., and where I somehow think he meets a gentleman like himself, and for all I know, ladies, and makes himself a good companion. All I ever see him do in the hotel is look pleasant. I wrote a note to him one day asking him to come to my room but the "Director" came instead. His chauffeur, Franz, was, as I have said, an S.A. (Sturm Abteilung) a special organization of loyal Nazis for political dirty-work. I dare say he could do the odd bit of espionage on the boss (or the boss on him—that is the system). Anyway as a hotel-keeper the proprietor was a good Nazi; and the chauffeur was probably good at something else besides chauffing. I had a letter from Franz after I left Bad Nauheim—not apologizing exactly, for not turning up to drive me to Heidelberg, but saying it was too bad I hadn't waited a little longer. Possibly he would just as soon have kept track of this stranger a little longer—just on general principles.

Not that there is anything dark or deep or Jesuitical about their procedures. It is on the contrary quite simple and direct—like Hitler's action in the case of the Roehm conspiracy. The average German wouldn't make much of a detective, though no doubt amongst seventy million people you could find some qualified sleuths. But the ordinary German has quite a capacity for minding his own business. It is when he is regimented and under orders that he becomes poisonous. What makes me think that of Franz is that as a S.A., which means that he is regimented, and he is the chauffeur of Herr Hilbert, a strong party man. I don't think that Herr H. would be at the head of a large hotel unless he was a good party man. These men must have a certain stand in, or with, the "Party." If you have such a stand-in you can do things that other men—or other women—cannot do. For there are women members of the party. I was told of one in Bad Nauheim, a Frau Dr. Kerber, wife of a doctor. I got her name from Dr. Herkel when I asked him about the place of women in the professions.[37] I expressed to him a desire to discuss the matter with a lady. He pursed his lips as much as to say that he was dubious of any such project. I don't know just where the dubiousness was directed but one thing is certain: Membership in the party is involved in an atmosphere of secrecy and cabal. Everybody recognizes that, but nobody at present takes offence at it—at least not openly. But wait: Is the German character so utterly impervious on the one hand to corruption and on the other to suspicion? What does it mean that everybody in Germany is so curious as to what one thinks of them in the Ausland. No Englishman would ask a German what the Germans thought of England. The German curiosity means at least that the thoughts of Germans are directed to comparative analysis of their own condition. Hitler, or somebody is now arranging to let the common people have their Volkswagen, an automobile to sell for about one-third the price of a Ford. When these Wagens begin to run around on the roads—the same roads as the big Mercedes-Benzes—certain questions and comparison will surely arise. Where will Gleichschaltung (sameness in rank) come in then?

I was discussing with Dr. Herkel one day the position of the Rotary Clubs in Germany. It appears that after being suppressed for a time, the Rotary Clubs have been allowed to go into operation again. The idea is that there must be no discussion of politics behind closed doors by a body of a closed membership. Apparently it had been determined that the Rotary Club was innocent enough and someone has given the high sign and allowed them to go ahead. But the corresponding club for business women, the Zonta Club, was still under the ban. I asked the doctor "When it comes to deciding on such a case, whether the club is to be allowed to operate or not, who makes the decision?" With the slightest curl of his lip he replied "Somebody in Berlin." In that curl of the lip lays the hope of democracy for Germany.

Actually, I suppose these things do sift down to some of the Germans. Hence Hitler's disquisition that democracy may be all right for some people but not for the Germans (which seems to amount to a kind of inferiority complex); and his and his exponents mocking at the "parliamentarizing" of other countries while the Germans drive straight at results. I am not denying that there is an argument there. I am simply speculating as to the state of mind of the German leaders who seem to find it necessary to indulge in gibes.

A fair way to judge material and economic and social progress and standards of living and that sort of thing is by observing the extent to which silk stockings are worn by the women. My observation so far seems to show as follows: Neither in Germany nor in France are silk stockings indispensable as they are in America. And when they are worn they need not be so thin or "sheer" as in America. They are, especially in Germany, usually quite substantial even if they are "sheer." In both countries there is quite a bit of lisle.[38] I would say that there are on the whole more silk stockings in Germany than in France. I am thinking, of course, of cities or places like Bad Nauheim and Royat, which are comparable. I am not thinking of country places. I am under the impression that in Germany the silk stocking is gaining ground faster than in France. In both countries there is a tendency on the part of those women who are young enough—and those who think they are young enough—to go without stockings. This is perhaps more noticeable in Germany where they take "movements" more seriously. There is no lack of style in Germany. Whether they follow Paris or not I am not in a position to judge.

It would also be both true and fair—as true and fair as such generalizations can be—to say that in Germany the thing we call liberty is being stifled—choked—by prosperity and well-being. The prosperity and well-being are there for anyone to see. On the edges of the industrial cities are the commodious and to the Germans entirely desirable, apartment houses for the workingmen. Sufficiently near to them to be conveniently reached by a walk are the garden plots, one for each family. These plots are regularly and rectangularly supplied each with its little tool house, in which it seemed to me one could spend the night if one wished. Here the German Hausvater cultivates his vegetables or smokes his pipe—or more probably the wife does the cultivating. One talks over the boundary with one's neighbor. What if the plot is small—about forty by fifty feet, it seems to me. One is just like one's neighbor. Gleichschaltung (sameness in rank) takes the place of the liberté of the Frenchman and the Englishman. Imagine Englishmen in those gardens! That, by the way, seems a rather new idea in politics. It doesn't somehow sound quite real—making people so happy that they don't want to be free. It is a thing that in the ordinary course of human nature just isn't done. And all the world has learned to treat the idea with incredulity. I suppose it is within the bounds of imagination that Hitler, Goering and Goebbels are spending their lives to make Mary-Lizzie happy. But you could not keep Americans from replying to such a supposition with "Oh Yeah." French people know themselves well enough to repudiate such an idea, except for purposes of intensive political eloquence. But the Germans are falling for it—this selling of their liberty for a mess of their own pottage. Hitler is wonderful. He is attributed with many of the qualities of divinity. His people do not see any feet of clay. Perhaps we should not anticipate. Perhaps the Germans will show the world something new in human nature. Some Germans contend that theirs is a real democratic system. Hitler is there by the vote of the people. He is doing what the people want. What more could anyone ask?

The word Gleichschaltung is a bit hard to translate. It presents the picture of a company of soldiers closely drawn up. Gleichschaltung implies that the ranks are perfectly straight, no one soldier standing farther forward or farther back than the rest. In the early days of Nazism Gleichschaltung used to be the order of the day. You don't hear so much of that now. Of course it means also what we would call in English "closing of the ranks." And that includes such ideas as excluding the Jews. But enough was said about it to sink it into the German mind. See if it does not come out presently in some disputable form. Could any government prevent a discussion of the question whether a Volkswagen should wait for a member of the Party to pass. Questions similar to that were of sufficient importance before the War to prevent the formation of social clubs in Germany as we have them in France or Anglo-Saxon countries. It seems safe to say that they will not prevent the use of the Volkswagen on the Autostrasse. Then what?

For nothing is clearer than that the present system involves, implicitly if not explicitly, an officer class, a ruling class, a "somebody in Berlin" as Dr. Herkel put it. Those "somebodys" are to be found as members of the party in small numbers in every fair-sized community. And they undoubtedly enjoy certain perquisites or privileges— power and prestige, if nothing else. They are not elected. They are selected by somebody somewhere. They are feared. They have their relationship with the secret police. Is that going to work out?

In Germany and Italy the one man selects himself and then asks for a vote, not of the representatives of the people selected from geographical divisions, but of the whole body of people (excluding the women, as it happens). To the abandonment of the geographical electoral divisions perhaps no insuperable objection can be made in principle, though there are objections. It is rather to the method of securing what appears to be public support that the objection lays. In the first place there must be no discussion or advocacy of any alternative. There must be no other party than the government party. All there is to do is to vote yes or no to the question, "Do you want this government?" That, in the nature of things and without any necessity of demonstration makes it practically impossible (to secure I was going to say, but that would imply that somebody, some leader wanted it; and there can be no such adverse leader) rather to produce an adverse one. Add to that the muzzling of the press, censorship of the mails and the operations of a secret police and you have a government practically proof against criticism or adverse vote no matter what it does.

The German method bows every individual voter to the yoke of tyranny. It is the ultimate Gleichschaltung. The extraordinary—the unspeakable thing is, that the ordinary German, in the street or elsewhere sees nothing wrong with this method of voting. If you gather up your nerve and mention it to him, and say for example, "How could you expect a real expression of opinion in Austria with such a ballot?" He looks at you with a mild surprise and says: "But everybody knew what the people wanted." And he may add: "If Schuschnigg had taken a vote the ballot would be valid just as much the other way." What can you do with such people? They would not see anything queer in what I have just said.

The whole idea is to fight the War over again. They don't admit it even to themselves, but that is what it amounts to. Suppose they got colonies—to satisfy their vanity—then what? They want to be military for the sake of militarism itself. It is their life. Individuals of course— many of them—depreciate war, but it seems as if the Volk as a whole would not know what to do with itself without its soldiering. After the War, while the rest of the world went about its business of trying to be happy, the German people were lost, not so much because of defeat, but because they had been deprived of their army. All you need to do to appreciate what happened is to see what is going on in Germany today as a common place matter; the glorification of militarism for its own sake. The attitude of the soldier, and particularly the officer, on the street, the sheep-like acquiescence, if not secret pride, of the civilian population, the marching, in rank and file, of young boys and girls, and over all the sentimentality, so blind that it is not even hypocritical—about "peace," where there is no peace.

Things like that you could say in Germany without any particular feeling of restraint. One would not expect that any umbrage would be taken. It is not like saying something against Hitler or failing to say "Heil Hitler"—or above all things saying something favourable to the hated Franzosen [French] or the Jews. The thing is to fight and destroy the hated French. And they will go on aggravating the French over one thing or another until they start something. The "politik" in the meantime is to get the French isolated. It may be that the Russians will yet save the world for peace.

While the Austrian Empire lasted the Czechs (Bohemians) were under the heel of the Germans. Now that the Czechs ... are in ascendancy within the boundaries or what always was Bohemia, the Germans who still live there "can't take it." That is the Czecho-Slovakian problem.

The Germans will not shick themselves drein with the other people of the world. The very principle which they espouse, or gleichschaltung they repudiate as between themselves and others—when others are on top. Thus there is no logic behind the German policy—except the logic of force. The policy of Germany is essentially the display and use, when necessary or possible, of force, as opposed to logic and reason. Logic, to a German is a process of justifying a conclusion which he has already espoused for sentimental reasons which do not submit to the test of logic. It is like history to a theologian. It teaches him nothing.

*There is one fundamental thing in our relations and
communications with Germany and Germans that is the cause of a
basic misunderstanding—a misunderstanding that frustrates most
of our efforts at coming to a better understanding. It is this: to us
it is the logical and just thing that Germany and Germans should
be punished for starting the War. But we are too polite and too
decent to remind the Germans of this. Our attitude is: "Why bring
that up?" Even I, with all my "frankness" never once got around to
that. The Germans of course only go so far as to consider that as
losers they had to pay a certain penalty. I know that Englishmen with
their faculty for slopping over and letting by-gones be by-gones are
utterly opposed to raising the point. But even with them it is basic.
The trouble is that the Germans don't understand this. They do not
realize, as every Englishman does, that you sometimes have to get
along with people you don't agree with. The Germans for example
have no thought of getting along with the French. And so friendliness
on the part of the English is misunderstood—that is to say by the
great body of the German people. They are a confiding sentimental
folk. If you get friendly with them they think you are just like they
are—ready to take on Hitler and Nazism and hate the French. The
very fact that they fall for this business of Gleichschaltung show the
essential difference between their mentality and ours. They tend to
be 100 per cent whatever they are. See how they vote "Ja."*

*I don't see myself how they can be got along with unless they
are taught the fundamental principle that being friendly does not
mean agreement, and that while we don't keep saying it, we keep on
holding them responsible for the War and for militarism. Also that we
appreciate the irony of our having fought so hard to attain democracy
for them, when they were not fit for it.*

*The Germans, as well as some other people (I might as well be
frank and say the people of the United States) fail to understand
that wonderful quality of the English for which there is no one
word. It consists of such ingredients as hospitality, kindness,
graciousness, consideration, gentleness and, in short, goodness.
Perhaps the shortest way to say it is gentlemanliness—or, let us
say, the quintessence of the Golden Rule. It is the thing that so
amazes the American (including the Canadian) on his first visit to
England. He finds himself in a maze—an atmosphere entirely new
to him. It is the sort of thing that makes people like the Lindbergs
want to live in England. It is the thing that makes rabid pro-German*

writers in the United States tear their hair. It more or less gets papers like the Toronto Star—and gets their goat. It is something perfectly palpable and well-recognized, though it is not often spoken of.

To do them justice, the United Statesans get the idea more quickly than anyone else—even Canadians. And they fall for it harder—to the chagrin of the 100 per cent Americans.

If you treat Germans as if they are social equals, they expect to go on, on that basis. I suppose it is too much to expect that they should recognize that they are not up to snuff. It wouldn't be human nature. We Canadians get used to the fact that Britishers can exhibit the soul of hospitality and yet reserve to themselves an inner sanctuary to which we do not belong—because we are from America if for no other reason. We don't resent it. We realize that British hospitality and goodness are so broad that there is plenty for us consistently with their right to reserve something for themselves. And living alongside the United Statesans and seeing ourselves to be so like them we don't blame the British from keeping something for themselves. How we grit our teeth at the strident nasal tone of the United Statesans, and hate ourselves for talking like them. And that is only one item.

But the German, basking in the gentleness of the Englishman, forgets his own crudeness and proceeds to act as if he belonged to the family—which makes it rather bad.

Have I said something? Have I said too much?

Reader, I can't tell a lie; I wrote some of the above quite a while after the date at the head of it.

I think I have at last found the ground solid under my feet with respect to these people [Mennonites] who have intrigued me for so many years. If there is any room for the use of brains in connection with religion (and I don't insist that there is); if there is any place for logic or probability (and I don't insist on that, for so great an authority as Saint Augustine said it was precisely because it was absurd and improbable—or words to that effect—that he was prepared to believe; in other words, there is no virtue in faith unless it is in the improbable); then I must come to certain conclusions. One of them is that if any religious body has a right to claim that it is perpetuating or carrying forward the Christian religion as established by its founder, that these people have that right. Another is that

*the body known as the Roman Catholic Church has gathered such
an enormous weight of corruption and false practice and belief
that there isn't a chance of its having any such right; though there
are now, as there have been down through the ages, individuals—
many individuals—who have adhered to that body and who have
nevertheless qualified as members of Christ's Church. Another
conclusion is that the so-called High Church in the Anglican body,
to the extent that it relies upon a real or fancied unity with the body
of which the Bishop of Rome is Primate, condemns itself to being
non-Christian—at least insofar as the Roman Catholic Church has
become corrupt and non-Christian. They can't have their cake and
eat it—or whatever is the proper wisecrack. The rest of the Anglican
Church to the extent that it regards sacerdotal practice as a mere
shell representing that useful British tendency to compromise on
non-essentials, gets by, on the equally useful principle of "all things
to all men." The Methodists, Presbyterian, Congregational and
Baptist bodies get by to the extent that they drop any insistence
on being in a superior position to bodies like the Mennonites. The
Congregational Church apparently would be okay. So where are we?
Are we all to go back and be Amish? Or would that be going back?
Or how much of it should we go back to? How much is a man entitled
to know and still be a Christian? Should there be a "Know-Nothing"
party in the church as there once was in American politics? These
questions get a bit thick, don't they? And there is no use sticking
your head in the sand and pretending the questions are not there.
To be a good Christian has a man got to be a good sand-sticker?*

Geneva, Switzerland. June 7, 1938

*I think this is as good a place as any to rest a day and catch up with
my correspondence. For one thing I have been turning over in my
head some things I would like to say to Richard Lichti—ostensibly
by way of answering his question as to what the Ausland thinks of
Germany. He had kept me up half the night telling me what ought to
be thought about Germany. I didn't feel I owed it to him to spare his
feelings. I found my text—indeed most of what I wanted to say—in
an article which I found at Wissembourg the morning after I had
got out of Germany, in a paper called* La Republique, *published in
Strasbourg[39]... I have had recourse to the Berlitz School to supply
me with a stenographer who can write German and French and can*

check up on my deficiencies in those languages[40]*.... I dictated an earful for Richard Lichti.... Separately from the letter I sent the article.... Let us see what the Post Office authorities of the Third Reich make of that.*

After various pleasantries and news not included here, Wegenast wrote as follows.

Dear Mr. Lichti, First I want to thank you once more for the great kindness and hospitality with which you received me, a stranger in a strange land....

The first newspaper I got crossing the border reminded me of you. It contained quite a concise answer to the questions that you put to me, about foreign opinion on German policy.

If you had not discussed this matter with me quite so freely, I should not risk sending you even this newspaper.

There is danger in it, too, as they would not voluntarily allow the paper to cross the border. I shall be circumspect and send you the newspaper separately. In case you should not receive it, will you please let me know.

The fact that it is so difficult to convey to Germans the opinion abroad, is of importance, too; but perhaps that isn't essentially the point.

The article will offend you, but one thing—and that is, so to speak, the only thing—I want to tell you, that is, that the article represents quite accurately foreign opinion. Naturally it doesn't contain everything that is being thought abroad, but everything that it contains is being thought abroad—that is to say, in all foreign countries, i.e. with the exception of Italy and Japan and minor parties in smaller states. In the United States, for example, not 1/10 per cent of those who think about these things, think differently from the article. Even in England it is quite well known that Mr. Chamberlain is playing the indulgent father....

Well, that is after all rather important, isn't it?—that in the world, which is becoming continually smaller, there is no room for the two; fascism and democracy. What is to be done? Are the English and the Swiss, and even the Irish to give up their democracy? I think I told you how in Innsbruck they were marching up and down the street singing: "Today Germany belongs to us, tomorrow the whole world." That's it. Where is it to end? Where in Czechoslovakia? Where in Switzerland? Where in Denmark? Where in Russia? And for how long?

Well, is one always to yield, because Germany wants this and that, one after another? Do the German people think that it can really go on so? Why is England arming now as never before? Why is the United States arming as never before? In view of this, is it necessary to say what the logical and inevitable results will be. Why does not Germany understand that? Or does she understand that?

I assume, of course, that it is possible that the whole outside world must be annihilated by the fascist countries—that democracy must die out in the world. That may be, but not without opposition. And that is the fact that I really wanted to present to you.

Personally, of course, you know that I have a very friendly feeling toward you, and personally you will not be offended, as I too, was not offended by your expression of opinion. Things are as they are; we didn't make them so.

Yours respectfully.

Wegenast added the following thoughts to his diary.

Prussia organized this political, military and philosophical system, and Italy gradually followed her.... How is it possible ... to cooperate with a state that continually wants only to take; that believes that if it has been granted one concession it can therefore demand further concessions; that never rests and never allows others to rest? ... Here, indeed, tragedy begins, tragedy for Europe and for the world. Prussianism demands more and more; knows no moderation and no bounds.... In contrast with this world, governed only by unbridled lust for power, driven and tormented by the insatiable greed for land, stand the world of democracy, in which the struggle for power is restrained and regulated by right.... It seems perfectly arguable that the greatest tragedy of all time was the betrayal of the League of Nations by the United States. But for that there would have been no Abyssinian war, no war in China, no rape of Austria, no Czechoslovakian crisis, and but for that it would not be necessary to have another war. And that betrayal was democracy in full operation. The people (of the U.S.) can do no wrong.

Much of Wegenast's focus in the diary between June and when he left in July related to the architecture of cathedrals in France, and to some extent in Britain. He also wrote extensively about the Catholic Church in relation to Protestantism. He continued, however, to talk to people wherever he went. The passages below serve as examples.

Royat, France. June 14th, 1938
A little piece farther on there was a large flock of sheep beside the road in charge of the shepherd and his dogs. Two sheep had begun to fight and one of the dogs stopped them. I stopped and had a talk with the shepherd, glad to find I could converse with an Auvergnat.... As the flock wandered on one ewe was left behind with her new-born

baby. The dogs were rounding up the rest of the sheep but paid no attention to her whatever, nor she to them. I told the old boy about my sheep at home and the ewe that had had three lambs each of three years in succession and brought them up. He agreed it was unusual—that they always pushed the third one away when they had three. (Not necessarily the third in point of time, as I have found out.)

Every flock I see in this country has a good percentage of black ones. And there is a type of black sheep, which I see often, with a white spot on the top of its head. I saw some in Switzerland.... I told the shepherd I had to feed my sheep all winter and I supposed he would have pasture the year round. He said, no, they had to feed all winter. I asked him what they fed. He said hay and (I think) the branches of certain shrubs or trees. I can believe the latter because I have to prevent the sheep from gnawing the bark off. Sheep will always leave the grass to eat the leaves of trees.

Royat-les-Bains, France. June 17, 1938
Presently into the bar came two peasants, one bare-footed, with a couple of sheep dogs. I got into conversation with them over the dogs, and soon we were great friends. The one who had shoes on showed me where his farmstead was a couple of rifle-shots away to the south. He said he had 280 hectares, which would be nearly 700 acres. I don't know whether he owns it or just has grazing rights. I did not see any land under cultivation. As far as the eye can see over the hills there are no trees. The soil seems extraordinarily rich in humus and to an unusual depth.... The poor old boy was quite deaf, which made conversation difficult.... He wanted me to come over to his place for tea the next time I was up. He said the patronne (wife) would make me a good cup of tea. He made several essays to treat me to beer but I told him it was defendu by my docteurs.

Fountainebleau. Evening, June 29, 1938
Reached here about ten o'clock and thought I might as well stay here tonight and go on in the morning.

I made good time all the way from Royat. The road was excellent, especially after I reached the national road which runs from Lyon to Paris.

I went by way of Vichy to get a drink of water at the source. It was worthwhile. That would be a good place to stay. The place is full of hotels.

The cattle in this district are practically all white. For fifty miles I did not see a beast other than white, and in the next fifty miles less than a dozen. The cattle suggest the Park cattle of England, which are supposed to be the original wild stock.

The land is mostly of the same chalky character that I noticed east of Reims. This year it has been very dry. The grain is very short—the hay of course likewise.

Further back I saw a sign "Central Poultry Farm"—just like that. I don't think I have seen a single poultry farm on my trip. Nor have I seen a flock of pure bred poultry of any kind.

The Park, Chateau de Fontainebleau. June 30, 1938
This place, immediately opposite my hotel, is about as quiet and cool and pleasant a place as one could wish to see. If there were nothing else to do it would be lovely to sit here and write you, my Journal. But, instead, I must drive on to Paris....

There is still plenty of forest, not only in the Royal Park, but elsewhere, north and south of Fontainebleau. I don't see how the French have been able to keep their hands off it....

The French realize the charm of eating and living out of doors. A café would get very little business in the summer even in the country places if it did not have tables out in front, on the sidewalk, or even on the street. There these Frenchies sit, pretending to sip some drink; but mostly they just "set." The Germans were on to it too; but they learned it from the Latins.

Paris. Evening, June 30, 1938
Back in the Hotel du Périgord for the night after various little errands and, for lack of anything better to do, a couple of hours at the zoo, where I had tea.

Calais to Dover, on the ferry. July 2, 1938
First shot out of the box I run into a pair of "Americans" from "America." They are at the table where I have sat down for a couple of sandwiches and a glass of milk. Oh joy, real bread, the first in three months and a half. I did not have any lunch but a bag of cherries. I was too crowded for time.... I had only just enough time to get the boat without going to Vimy. But I thought I must take the risk. I had lunch. I ran into the Warden himself the moment I arrived at the entrance to the Canadian trenches. He was George H. Stubbs,

formerly of Winnipeg. (He ventured he was a namesake but not
a relative of a celebrated jurist.) Mr. Stubbs interested himself
personally in seeing that I saw as much as possible during the few
minutes I could spare.

The Canadian trenches will be there for a long time for the future
generations to see. The story of the blowing up of Vimy Ridge and the
advance of over four miles into the open country beyond is one of
the epics of the War. I had no idea that the craters were so large or
that the operations had been on such an enormous scale.

There were no signs in Arras for a long distance beyond [sic]
announcing Vimy. It was only by constant questioning that one found
one's way though everyone knew where Vimy was. I remarked on
this to Mr. Stubbs.... It appears that there is competition for the
attention of tourists and the French are disposed to be jealous of the
amount of attention which Vimy is getting in comparison with places
like Notre Dame de Lorette [a French national cemetery]. Mr. Stubbs
wants me to take the matter up at Ottawa.

I caught the boat, but my car was the last to go on.

Canterbury, England. July 3, 1938

I had to round out my career of church-going on this trip by
attending, in the crypt of Canterbury Cathedral, a Huguenot service
in French conducted by a Methodist minister from Canada, and at
the close of the service, at the request of the minister, playing on
the organ (in the church) manufactured at Clinton, Ontario.... It came
about on this wise:

Visiting the Cathedral late yesterday afternoon, I came across a
guide with a small party of tourists in the crypt, explaining, first, the
incident of the killing of Thomas-a-Becket, showing where he was
stabbed and where they laid him afterwards, etc. After that the guide
told about a chapel in the crypt where the Huguenots had continued
to hold services regularly since the time of Henry VIII, and that there
would be a service this afternoon. I asked him some questions and
elicited, amongst other things, that ... the refugees were granted the
right to hold their meetings in the crypt while mass was still being
said on the floor above. The French services in the crypt have been
going on continuously ever since—interrupted, I suppose, by the
reign of Queen Mary.

The present incumbent, Mr. Barnabas, has been there for
nearly forty years. He came from Montreal, where he had been doing

missionary work for the Methodists.... These things I learned from
Mr. Barnabas after the service, when I introduced myself to him.
The service, I have said, was in French. There were not many
there. There were some real Huguenots and some tourists like myself.

The last entry, extract below, was made on board ship bound for Canada.

Cherbourg, France. July 9, 1938
The gulls here are exactly the same bird as on the Great Lakes. The
coast of France, as I see it once more, is very green and pleasant
to the eye.... Coming out of the social atmosphere of England and
into this boat is an experience to be felt.... One could distinctly feel
the change on stepping on a Canadian ship. There was a hardness
in social relations—an insistence on social status and values which
the Englishman does not find necessary or proper. A Canadian thinks
it necessary to maintain an attitude of aloofness toward those whom
he wishes to excel socially. The Englishman feels no such necessity.

Little of Wegenast's correspondence with the people he met has survived—
that is letters that were written to him. The only letters written by him that
have survived are the one to Lichti which Wegenast included in the diary, and
the letter/notes to Sigfrid Schmidt that are dealt with in the next chapter. A
translation of the few written to him that still exist (outside those appearing
in the next chapter) are found below. Two are from Hans Müller, the young
boy who had admired Wegenast's car in Plankstadt. Some of what Hans has
to say makes little sense without Wegenast's letter; the reference to South
America, for example. One letter is from Richard Lichti. Wegenast had hoped
to hear from Lichti while still in Europe. Lichti, however did not respond until
Wegenast was back in Canada. Lichti's single letter was written in August
and addressed to Wegenast's Toronto office. The last two were written by
Mina and Josef Nafziger (members of a Mennonite family in Luxemburg) to
Wegenast's law partner, Margaret Hyndman, after Wegenast's death and at
the end of the war.

Plankstadt, June 9, 1938

Dear Mr. Wegenast,
I was pleased to receive your friendly letter and picture. I didn't think that you
would fulfil your promise and send me a picture. But after you kept your word I was
all the happier. I see that you, as a foreigner, have good memories of us, and that
you liked our Fatherland. Hopefully, we will look back happily on these times. I will

treasure the picture that you sent me and keep it in honour in the years ahead. I wish you all the best in the future and extend to you my warmest thanks.

Sincerely, Heil Hitler,

·   Hans Müller

Hans Müller   Plankenstadt, November 9, 1938

Dear Mr. Wegenast,

I was very pleased to receive your friendly letter of 18 October 1938. I see from it that you arrived home safe and sound, and that you are slightly surprised not to have heard anything from me about the picture that you sent. As you can see from the enclosed page 4, I had already written to you to Geneva. It would appear that you did not receive that letter. I am very pleased though once more that you remember me. I see from this that you are a good and honest man, and that it is important to you to hear from me again. I do this gladly. Excuse me when I humbly ask you where you are right now. I take it that you are in South America. And I know that it must be very warm there. On the other hand, I saw the word Canada on the postage stamp and I was confused because skating is a major sport there. However, I can't manage to bring this together in my mind: on the one hand it is warm but on the other there is lots of skating? At Easter, I'll graduate from school where I learned to use a typewriter, and I typed this letter with the typewriter. I would be very happy if you would send me your news: as you know, children are always a little curious. I hope that this letter finds you well and that you are thinking fondly of our German fatherland.

I close sincerely with the German salutation, "Heil Hitler," Hans Müller

Richard Lichti
Farmer
Neustadt an der Haardt
Branchweilerhof 10
28 August, 1938

Dear Mr. Wegenast,

Please forgive me for my great negligence in not having returned your great friendliness for so very long. All the work, official duties and worries are the reasons for this.

Above all, [accept] my personal thanks for all your friendly mail which you sent me while on your big trip, but also in the name of everyone here whom you met so very far from your homeland, [accept] the warmest greeting and thanks for the lovely pictures which you sent us. Especially old mother Lichti was very happy about that, since she had not really expected it. We all hope that you returned safely from your long trip, that you learned a lot on your trip, and that it will teach you much.

As to the political questions which I had put to you and which you attempted to answer in your letter as well as in the newspaper you sent—that was not really a satisfactory response, but this cannot and must not cloud our young and sincere friendship. Today, I cannot go into these matters in detail either, but I hope that I may be able to do so this winter. Perhaps future history will also help relatives and friends who live outside of Germany to understand the National Socialist world view, culture, and so forth.

Have you had some tangible success also in the genealogy research which you have done about Hege Lichti and so on?

I would be very happy indeed to hear something from you about this.

Herewith, I will close my letter and send the most sincere greetings from my family.

Your Richard Lichti.

Echternach, October 1, 1945

My dear Miss M. Hyndman,

Many thanks for your friendly words, though we were very sad to hear that our dear friend Wegenast no longer is alive. We had hoped to see each other after the war. We are so happy that we have the pictures of him that he took when he was here. Unfortunately, the letters that he so carefully wrote telling about his particular impressions and the photos that he included in them were lost in the war: the front part of the house was heavily damaged by bombs and the furniture and their content were blown out into the court.

I was very happy that you were so kind as to start exchanging letters with us in the name of our dear friend. I want to tell you a bit about our experiences: it is a year now since all the fuss started. We spent two weeks in the forest under a cliff because on the radio we were told by the English to stay away from the main roads and all means of transportation. Meanwhile, the Nazis stole from us everything they could carry away.

On 12 September 1945, we were able to breathe more easily because our liberators arrived in Luxembourg: that was good news. But we weren't yet part of the liberated because the Nazis were still in power where we were. We lived in the hope that our turn would also come but it didn't come as quickly as we had hoped.

Finally, the first American soldiers arrived: we would have embraced them all but that's when the worst part came. We had to move on because the soldiers needed accommodation, and they evacuated us. We went to the place of one of our brothers who had an empty house and stayed there two weeks. But then he had to move on with us too. We went on about 65km towards the Belgian border. When the Rundstedt Offensive came again, we had to move on for the third time, and the more we wandered, the less we had to carry. All that in the deep cold. It was not pleasant at all. On the 18 March we were able to return home. We were happy to do that, but it was with mixed feelings: we could imagine what it was like at home because we had heard on the radio that the fighting had been intense around Echternach and how many good young American soldiers had to lose their lives to free us from the Nazi plague. How can the little Luxembourg show its thanks to a big, rich country like America for everything it has done for us?

In any case, we could go home. We were disappointed: it was worse than we had imagined, but we were home. We too had to sacrifice something, too. We told ourselves, it doesn't matter, we are free of the Nazis. Then we got to work with our property. First, we had to make sure we got a roof on the house. That took awhile as I said earlier, but it got done. Thank God we had good weather in the spring so that we didn't feel the lack of a door and windows. Now things are much better: we have two rooms and the kitchen in order and can live in them. It's going slowly but it's improving. There are so many people who need help that things can't move along very quickly.

Now then my dear Miss Hyndman I've given you a little picture of the situation but it isn't anything happy that I am telling you about. I would be very happy and very thankful to you to receive another letter from you in memory of our dear friend Mr. Wegenast.

Very sincerely from Mina Nafziger

Perhaps we will have the pleasure, dear Miss Hyndman, to meet you personally once we have everything in order again. What do you think?

Echternach, 8 December 1945

My dear Miss Hyndman,

I take the liberty again of writing humbly to you at your address: in your lovely letter you so kindly offered us your help, but at the beginning I was embarrassed to approach you. However, our need is now greater than our shame and I would be very, very thankful if you chose to take this opportunity to help a bit. It is cold now and we lack so much for the winter: we need a heater. There is wood and coal for sale here but everything is so terribly expensive that we cannot afford it. A man's shirt costs, for example, 240 Francs, and this is leftover war material. In dollars that comes to about $5.50. Shoes cost 340 to 400 Francs, about $8–$8.50, a man's suit 9,000 to 10,000 Francs, that is about $295. A 1000 Francs fly from your hands in no time.

Otherwise, things are going better, the house is already somewhat liveable, if one isn't spoiled (that is something that we got rid of long ago). We are happy to have a roof over us, and everything is just about finished except for the garage: it still lacks a roof. Last week six men were working here but they had to stop for lack of material. That's understandable because so much material is being used, not only in Germany but everywhere in Europe.

The Americans are really doing a lot for little Luxemburg, we've heard that so much clothing has come into the cities. In the cities the need is much greater than in the country. But this is already being distributed in the country, too. It is truly moving what the USA is doing for us. We can't thank them enough, first of all for having freed us from the Nazis, and then from need. May God bless them for that.

With the greatest solidarity we send our greetings, dearest Miss Hyndman. Mina and Josef Nafziger.

We also send a hearty Luxemburger Greeting for the dear writer.[41]

THE SIGFRID SCHMIDT FILE

4

The trip left sad and lasting impressions on F.W. Wegenast. He could not get over his disgust for what he saw as the prevalent form of German thinking, as is evident from a thick file of yellowing papers he kept after returning home and which he named the Sigfrid Schmidt file. Wegenast provided the background behind the file, starting with his meeting of Sigfrid Schmidt, a young German living in France.

On the 5th May, 1938, as I drew up before the Cathedral in Reims, it occurred to me to have a snapshot of myself with the car in front of the Cathedral. I looked around for someone to take the picture, when I noticed a young man coming across the square. I walked up to him and explained what I wanted. He said he would be glad to take the picture; he had some experience with photography himself.... Then we got to talking about this and that. I judged by his accent that he was more familiar with German than with French, and addressed him in German. I had guessed right, and we continued our conversation in German. He had a job in Reims as a translator. He was much interested in my being from Canada. His ambition was to get to Canada or the United States. He asked me if I could give him any information about the country. I happened to have a C.P.R. folder in the glove-box of my car. The last two pages contained information about the C.P.R. Steamship lines. I tore these from the folder and gave them to him. He said he would have great difficulty getting away. His parents in Germany were well enough off, but they would not be allowed to supply him with the money. I judged he was one of those who would rather be out of Germany than in, and I talked to him on that basis.

Some months after I had got back to Toronto, I received a letter from him asking whether I remembered him, and how the snapshot had turned out.[1] I replied ... [and] my letter [dated December 15, 1938] contained several enclosures.... In due time I received a long letter in reply [dated December 26].... A good while afterwards I received another letter from him, asking for news, and suggesting among other things, that I might visit him at his home in Germany the following summer.[2] In the meantime I had made several essays at drafting a reply to the long letter of December 26th, which was in the nature of an exposition of the doctrines of the National Socialist party and a reply to my criticisms of Hitler's policy. But each time I made the effort I ended by thinking: "What is the use? This man is in France where he has all the facilities afforded by that country for getting himself straightened away. If he will not hear them neither will he be persuaded [through one] who wrote from Canada."

However, one Sunday when I was up to see my friend Aaron Laidlaw, shortly before he passed away, and found Mrs. Folkes, a red Russian literary woman, also on a visit, and we got to talking about Germany. I remembered that I had my draft attempts out in the car. I got them in and read them for Mrs. Folkes's benefit, and explained that I had given up the idea of sending them to Sigfrid Schmidt.... Aaron Laidlaw pulled himself together and said: "There is one thing I want you to promise me, Frank—that you will send that letter." So I promised. But before I could get the letter in shape the war broke out. And so here are the shreds dangling in mid-air:

Wegenast's letter, dated December 15, 1938, and sent to Schmidt, contained the following passages. It is not clear whether Wegenast wrote the letter to Schmidt in English or in German.

I have often thought of you and have mentioned you in some of my speeches. What struck me was your difficulty about getting away from Europe. I wonder if you would mind explaining that a little more. Shall I ask you some questions? What unpleasantness would there be if you took the boat and landed at Montreal or New York? Are you supposed to report to the German government before doing such a thing? Has the German Government any claim on you for military service? Would they punish you if you came back to Germany? May I ask you some more questions? In what work are you engaged in France? Does the German Government make any difficulties about letting you go to France? Are any particular conditions imposed on you?

I am curious about these things and people ask me about them. I have just read a book called "Assignment in Utopia" by Eugene Lyons. It is published in England. I think you would appreciate it. It speaks, amongst other things, of the extraordinary difficulties which anyone has in getting out of Russia. The principle impression the book made on me was that of the parallelism between Russia and Germany. The principle conditions are essentially the same: a dictatorship under which individual liberty and life and humanity and truth must give way to exigencies imposed on people for their supposed good.

As you are in France you must understand something of the sentiment against Germany outside its borders. I think you can have no idea how solid this sentiment is in the United States and Canada. It is precisely because of the lack of appreciation in Germany of the thing we call liberty, for which during four or five hundred years the Anglo-Saxon peoples have fought, that we are so distrustful of Germany. We would not break our heads over the *drang nach Osten* or any other form of German expansion if it did not mean the negation of liberty. And I am beginning to think it will be *einerlei*[3] if the Germans went in and cleaned up Russia. Hitlerism is not worse than Stalinism. It would give Germans something to amuse them, and a little soap and water wouldn't hurt the Russians. You get the idea of my talking to you like this? It is the sort of thing one hundred million people in America would say to one another. I thought it might interest you.

After I left you I went into Luxembourg and then into Germany where I put in about three weeks. I need hardly tell you the impression one gets on crossing the border. The German people are industrious and orderly and honest, and above all, clean. They are also kind and hospitable and good. But nevertheless each time I crossed the border out of Germany into France I had the feeling, "Thank God I am out of that." I think you know what it is like. To tell you the truth I have something like the same feeling, but only a very little, when I cross the border from Canada into the United States. One feels a little freer. People do what they like. Of course in the main it is that way with us. There is the difference between night and day between us (North Americans) and Germany. Nobody can put me into a concentration camp. The whole might of the courts and of public opinion would insist on my having a fair trial no matter what I was charged with.... The people there (the United States) respect the Law for its own sake. We, in Canada, have the advantage of having a Sovereign as well as the law. And it does make a difference. Our courts are more formal than those in the United States. The lawyers as well as the judges wear appropriate gowns and the procedure is more formal. I have never known an American who did not agree that that was an advantage.

However I have rambled on in this fashion to give you an idea of how a man in Canada thinks and talks. Now you must do the same for me....

Don't imagine I am trying to argue with you or propagandize. The Germans—and so far as that is concerned the French—can have their ideologies. What they can't do, so far as I am concerned, is to impose them on other parts of the world in which I am interested in.

The following is from the long letter, dated December 26, 1938, that Schmidt sent back in reply to Wegenast's December 15 letter. It is unclear whether or not Schmidt wrote in English or if Wegenast made this rough translation. The fact that Schmidt was training to be a translator, and the roughness of the English suggests that Schmidt wrote the letter in the English seen below.

Very Honoured Mr. Wegenast.
Your valued letter which to my surprise I received yesterday gave me much pleasure. This time, however, I should not like to have you wait a long six months for a reply.... First I will answer your questions.

1) In case that I should wish to travel to New York or to you in Toronto I should not have to fear the slightest unpleasantness of the part of the German government. Why should I?

2) Previously to ask permission at any German office is not necessary. I am in every respect free and can do what I like.

3) Although I did not have to perform my full military service, I am still liable for military service. As a German living abroad I am subject to the Central Office for reporting for defense of the War Ministry and am bound to report from time to time to this service post.

4) If I have fulfilled the duty under the third head I need not fear the least punishment if I return to Germany after a lengthy foreign stay.

5) I am staying in France in the meantime to complete my knowledge of the French language in order to prepare for my examination as a translator, which purpose taking in Berlin in the Spring of 1940. I am making my living here by translation work and by German teaching. My wife is working as an office secretary.

6) I am able to travel from Germany to France without any difficulty.

7) The only difficulty in undertaking a foreign journey consists in the obtaining of exchange, since one may, generally speaking, at the moment take out of Germany only ten marks per month. The reason for this measure is the German scarcity of exchange and gold. Foreign pleasure trips forbid themselves therefore for Germans for the time being. The ban on export of exchange, however, has nothing to do with tyranny as one always likes to represent it outside of Germany, but is dictated simply and solely by the duty of thrift.

Now some observations on the thoughts cited by you out of the book, "Assignments in Utopia" and on Bolshevism in general. I have myself never been to Russia and therefore do not know the Bolshevism of Mr. Stalin from experience. But one thing I can say not because it may be demanded by reasons of state or general well-being, but because a band of uncultured vagabonds wishes the downfall of the civilized world and is instigated from Moscow. Or the horror and inhumanity of the Russian bolshevism Russian emigrants have told me enough.

It is folly to attempt to seek parallels between National Socialism and Bolshevism. They are as different as fire and water. To demonstrate more closely that, and why, there is nothing in common between National Socialism and Bolshevism would lead too far in the framework of this letter. If you wish, however, dear Mr. Wegenast, I will lay this matter before you in detailed disquisition. Bolshevism is the offspring of a degenerate world-concept which has become meaningless and which is dying out. National Socialism, on the other hand, is the victorious world-concept of tomorrow. Reduced to its simplest formula one could say that National Socialism is a world-concept which realizes the return to the natural and God-given laws of life—eternal laws which holds the stupidly presumptuous rationalistic-materialistic world-concept of the last 150 years to be obsolete and useless. The consequences are everywhere to be seen clearly today.

Self-realization for each people in accordance with its biologic-natural gifts—its racial peculiarities, its tendencies of character and intellectual capacities are the requirements and fundamental principles of National Socialism. In its basic aspect this is nothing else than democracy. For this reason we Germans have no interest to carry our hides to the Soviet market. We do not wish to make any conquest in Russia. We do not wish to absorb either Poland or Czechoslovakia or Hungary or Romania. Whoever says that is a fool. We want a Kingdom of Germans and a national and individual life suitable to our genetic and racial characteristics. National Socialism is not imperialistic but Bolshevism is. Its lust of conquest and overthrow in all lands demonstrates this sufficiently.

To National Socialism it is in principle immaterial what form of state or world concept a non-German state acknowledges. An example: If Bolshevism were to attempt to bolschevise Canada National Socialism would on the contrary abstain from any attempt to influence, knowing fully that it would be useless and senseless to try to force upon Canadians conditions and views other than those natural to them. "Everyone can obtain salvation in his own fashion"; to this maxim of the great Prussian king, Frederick II, Adolf Hitler also adheres. Now, yet a few words on the theme "freedom": I concede quite openly, dear Mr. Wegenast, that the English and French people are freer than the German people at this time. But understand me rightly: if one has pulled the reins a little more tightly on the German people it is not to bring them under servitude but to train them. The German folk is becoming today what the English and French have long been—a nation. And to weld together a people in all its opposing parts often requires severe measures—a strict training. Half-measure will not obtain this end. However, the best proof is the history of the English people and its empire. First the hard hand of the leaders of the British people gave to the English people its oneness, its stamp. And it had to shed streams of blood before it became a nation..

Adolf Hitler is a similarly greater former [*sic*]. He fulfills the yearnings of all Germans for centuries: one realm, one people.

The times when the Germans were satisfied with the beautiful title of "folk of Poets and Thinkers," when they split into thousands and thousands of groups and grouplets, made war over trifles, wasted their strength in fratricidal conflicts or stood inactive or powerless while other peoples made themselves masters of the world or arbitrated their conflicts of interest on the broad back of the German folk are once and for all past. Hardly five years ago one still evinced one's pride in Germany, to be Prussian, Bavarian, Württemberger, Thuringian or such like. Even in passports for foreign countries the description "Nationality, Prussian" was used. Ridiculous! Today, thank God, that has disappeared. In order that it should disappear, for the benefit of all, the reins had to be pulled a little tighter, to bring reason to the eccentrics of who there were in Germany not a few. Outside of Germany, and in particular in France which was the greatest beneficiary of German dissension and therefore conceivably had and perhaps still has the greatest interest therein, the very appropriate political training is characterized as a dictatorship.

"I am British" an Irish lady once indignantly replied to my question whether she was Irish. Everywhere in the British Empire one can hear this answer as in Canada, Australia, Scotland and elsewhere. When for the Germans this wholesale spirit of unity and harmony has been attained, the bridle will certainly be taken off the German people. I hope, dear Mr. Wegenast, that you will rightly understand my exposition and that I am expressing myself clearly enough. I am compressing myself as much as possible and am limiting myself to a few examples. I leave it to you to deduce from these other similar or parallel ones.

The institute of this great popular-national development is the Party. Every young German is taken up automatically as a member of the Hitler Youth on the completion of his eighteenth year. That one has in such times of training and with a view to a great common purpose, to forego one's own particular desires, mostly unimportant, has nothing whatever to do with oppression. It is not true that we Germans are groaning under the knout. We obey with willing obedience. We see in Adolf Hitler our chosen leader. We serve his cause because he has freed us Germans from the servitude of strangers, because he gave back to the German people its honour, its freedom, its work and its bread, because he has made his people strong and unassailable, because he strives to create for the broad masses of the people a life of beauty and social justice, because he wishes a glorious, healthy, beautiful, sport-steeled youth as the heirs of the realm, because he is building his great, imperishable culture which is uniting itself worthily to those of our old masters. Who would, therefore, call him a dictator or even a contemptible tyrant. We serve him because he is himself our first servant; we follow him because we love him; we work for the continuation of his work because of innate, lofty inspiration. Not in the fulfillment of our folkish laws. To attain such a great aim a long period of peace is needed. We Germans do not want war; we do not glory it; we know that misery, hunger, downfall follows in its train.

You can rely on my words, dear Mr. Wegenast, more than those of the odious and stupid newspaper writers. I am writing here in Reims, and am therefore completely free and uninfluenced; I do not stand, as one might perhaps say, under duress; no man controls my interests. I would have many more things to say and to put right; but I will here limit myself to the most needful; the letter is already too long.... A little correction yet: The song you heard in Innsbruck was not "Today we own Germany and tomorrow it will be the whole world," but "Today Germany hears us," etc.

Very honoured Mr. Wegenast, I should be very glad if we could continue this exchange of views regularly in a sort of "political letters." To clash spears in knightly combat steals. By our exchange of view we will contribute to the improvement of the reciprocal relations in the lives of the peoples. That is a noble and beautiful task. In the hope of an early reply and with hearty New Year's wishes for your personal prosperity, very honoured Mr. Wegenast, I greet you.

Wegenast never answered this letter, although he wrote a draft response dated January 12, 1939. It was this draft that Wegenast read to Laidlaw and promised to finish and send to Sigfrid. The following passages are from that document.

If it were possible to transplant into your mind what I thought of each of your observations there might be some object in my undertaking to reply to you. But if your living in France for months or years has not given you insight I cannot hope to do so in a letter. Also (and this is a thing which I find few, if any Germans understand), one must be a gentleman, and a gentleman does not say things that would have to be said to make you understand.

And so I suppose you will go on to the end of the chapter failing to understand. The whole thing is so pitiful—so erbarmlich.[4] *I understand everything in your letter perfectly. I understand your state of mind, your attitude, your philosophy, your* Weltanschauung. *You do not understand me at all. You understand certain words and sentences but the most important things I know (and many others know) ... you do not know at all. Your mind is in fact conditioned against knowing these things. It is something like a religion with you. You would regard it as a* temptation—versuchung[5]—even to entertain the idea that what 130,000,000 people in America think might be correct.

That is the way Germans are, and in that they are distinguishable from the rest of the world. And that is notwithstanding the fact that a few years ago there was no Nazism and a few years before that the same people who now shout for Hitler shouted for the Kaiser. If you cannot see the parallelism, not to say similarity, between the principles and techniques of Stalinism on the one hand and Hitlerism on the other, what can one do but give you up? And what can the rest of the world do with the Germans but fight them or convert them somehow?

The hopeful thing, of course, is that they are so susceptible to change. The theory they espouse today is forgotten or repudiated tomorrow. But one never knows what damage they will do while they are running blindly in a certain direction. It is that way about the facts in connection with the commencement of the War in 1914. It is that way about the theory of a Teutonic race. And so on indefinitely. Perhaps the greatest lack in the German character is the one to which reference is so often made in the Ausland, namely, that the German has no sense of humour.... The lack of it is a tragedy for the Germans and the rest of the world, because it is obvious now that the conflict is unvermeidlich.[6] And of course you have seen (the people in Germany probably have not seen) how the United States has finally got into its stride. We Canadians felt rather bitterly the slowness of the United States to get into the last war. Our losses were as great as those of the United States and we considered we were fighting the battles of the United States until they came in. They will not be so tardy this time. Indeed the only way a self-respecting Briton can reconcile himself to the advent at Munich is by considering that for once the British were wise enough to wait for the United States....

It is a most extraordinary thing and a reflection on the human intellect that it can be kept from the people of Germany that Hitlerism inevitably leads to a life-and-death struggle with democracy. The liberties which the Anglo-Saxon people and the French people have enjoyed for one hundred and fifty years will not be surrendered to the exigencies of totalitarianism. We will not give up personal freedom or freedom of the press or freedom of speech for the Gleichschaltung which Russia and Germany find necessary to attain what their leaders think desirable. We in America did not need Gleichschaltung to get us where we are. Why do the Russians and Germans think they need it in order to attain our way of living—which, I think you will admit, compares favourably with any in Europe. The great gift of the Anglo-Saxon people to the world (for it was born in England, not the United States or France) is the thing called "liberty," which the democratic people live and die for and which the totalitarian people spit on.

But how can one reason with people who do not see the similarity of Russia and Germany in this respect. It is of course a fact that National Socialism fell heir *to and absorbed the strong Communist element which threatened to overwhelm Germany before the advent of Hitler. There are differences between Germany and Russia, between the Germans and the Russians, but in this one thing over which the conflict will inevitably come the Russians and the Germans are in the same boat. They submit to the same kind of discipline; and the leaders use the same technique. And the rest of the world will not stand for it.*

So there we are. And instead of making you understand what I am saying, you will try to make me understand something which I understand perfectly well. You must remember that we have access here to all thought and all information. We make mistakes and we may have wrong ideas, but amongst several hundred million people there are always some who will sooner or later point out our mistakes. Another thing. You have talked to me about coming to Canada or the United States. The only Germans who are welcome in either country are those who either travel through the country to see things for themselves or those who are prepared to settle down and forget they are Germans and become loyal citizens of the country in which they live. There is no place either in Canada or the United States for a German to settle down and remain German.

After speaking to Laidlaw about pursuing the correspondence, Wegenast returned to work on this draft, but he found the whole thing as difficult to deal with as when he had earlier abandoned the thought of responding. For Franklin agonized over the whole thing—the beliefs of the young man, the state of Germany, and the racial thinking behind so much German perception of events. Franklin loathed Hitler, and noted that not one American in a thousand understood how bad the situation in Germany was. Few had read *Mein Kampf*. He claimed that only French versions carried the entire original contents of the book, and that many English translations were purged or sanitized revisions.[7] He rehashed British history in his notes, wondered how he could convert Sigfrid from his devotion to Hitler. Wegenast's obsession with British culture, and biased points of view on the subject were as strong as his anti-German feelings. He filled literally hundreds of handwritten pages, written in both German and English. Sometimes he would dash off a thought in a few lines on a page and add it to the file. Sometimes he wrote out long passages concerning history and religion. There is much repetition in the material, because it remained so unorganized. In the end, Wegenast did not pull together a letter to send to Schmidt before war made such an effort senseless. But he kept the thick file. Some of the main themes in Wegenast's thoughts from these handwritten notes are included here.

Germans seem to think themselves entitled to make it miserable for the rest of the world. "That which is the object of our fight is to assure the existence and development of our race and our people; it is to nourish its children and to conserve the purity of blood of liberty and the independence of the fatherland so that our people may ripen for the accomplishment of the mission which is destined for it by the Creator of the universe," [wrote Hitler].

On this sentence [from the original version of Mein Kampf] certain questions protrude: why our race and our people? Are the others to be ignored or brushed aside or destroyed? Is there to be a philosophy or a line of argument that is good for the Germans but not good for other races or peoples? Preserve the purity of blood? What blood? What purity? The German people are the people who have learned to speak the German language. They are a mixture in which the Alpine predominates. They may be Aryan but the term "Aryan" has reference to language not race. They are for the most part not Nordic like the Danes and Norwegians. What Nordic blood may be in them (and some ethnologists say there is practically none) comes by way of the Danes and Norwegians and Friesians. The Prussians are a Baltic race with a large infusion of Mongolian. The blond hair and blue eyes are in large measure from Slavic sources, though there are strains of Scandinavian and Finnish. The idea of the Germans as pure "Nordic" is a pure myth.

And who was interfering with the "liberty" or "independence" of the fatherland? Why does Germany need a different kind of liberty? Because Germany wants it. Or because some German leaders want it. Is there any other reason that can be cited to a non-German? ... Then what "mission"? And is the Creator to be given a hand in determining the mission? ... Did the same creator to whom Herr Hitler for the moment gives recognition by any chance create the Jews? If the Jews are to be punished for repudiating Jesus what should be done to Rosenberg and Goebbels and Streicher?[8]... What a ridiculous mess this whole Nazi business is. And to think that such mental acumen as human beings possess should have to be spent in exposing its fallacies.

The idea of a young man or boy spending his physical energy with the objective of fitting himself to kill his fellow men is so horrible that any decent normal mind recoils from it. But that is what the German youth is taught. And effort is made to reconcile the women to the idea. Deliberately their minds are being directed to the task of bearing sons to die in battle for the Fatherland. (The daughters do not seem to matter except as bearers of more sons.)

*There is much in your letter that is admirable. You are
intellectually, I think, capable of shaking loose from the fetters
and falsehoods of Nazism. And you have a background of general
knowledge which, with some enlightenment, would enable you
to supply the correctives yourself. You have, for example, some
knowledge of English history and you seek to draw parallels. But
in essential points you are quite wrong. The English did not attain
unity first and then liberty. If that is Hitler's idea it would be wrong,
but I think he would repudiate your suggestion that Germans
should ever have liberty of the English kind. The English were
always individualists, and always resisted arbitrary authority. Back
in the reign of Stephen, within half a century after the Norman
conquest, when at a great Council of the people (Note that the
"parliamentarism" which Hitler despises was in full operation then)
it was proposed to introduce Roman law. The people rose and with
one voice shouted, "We will not have anything but the laws of the
English." A hundred years later came Magna Carta. It was all down
through the centuries. Freedom, justice and equality before the law
were demanded by the individual Englishman, and those rulers who
were not wise enough to give in lost their thrones, and sometimes
their heads. That is the difference between the Englishman and the
German. Hitler himself points out how the German learned to bow
and scrape to his king and he exhorts him to stand up for himself.
That is what the Anglo-Saxon learned to do a thousand years ago.*

*The Anglo-Saxons seem to have learned something from the
Danes. For the Danes perfected parliamentary institutions before
the Anglo-Saxons did. In 1930 the people of Scotland celebrated
the 1000th anniversary of the establishment of their Alking or
parliament.[9] The Germans are at least 1000 years behind their
Nordic neighbours in democratic institutions. The English of course
had their Witanagemot twelve or thirteen hundred years ago. They
brought it from Germany, but not from Prussia. No, you are quite
wrong in your ideas of English history and the development of the
English spirit of freedom.*

*You say: "Im ritterbicken Kamff die klingen zukreuzen, stählt."
But who wants in this day and age to be steeled? The Germans,
not the English, not the Americans, not the French. If they steel
themselves, as they did in 1914–18 and are doing again, it
is because they propose once and for all to stop this steeling
business—or perish in the attempt. I, and many like me, would*

119

*rather die than live in a world where steel and German Schroffheit
rules supreme. We have no word in English for this thing which you
call in German völkish,[10] just as you have no word for the English
idea of "gentleman." The most tolerant people in the world are the
English; the most intolerant are the Germans.[11] Hence the success
of the English as colonizers and the failure of the Germans. The
peoples of the world are appalled and disgusted with the German
attitude towards other peoples, e.g. the Jews. Many of us dislike
Jews and Negroes and Japanese etc. It is natural, perhaps. But one
of our tasks as civilized beings is to control those dislikes. We must
be gentlemen; we must be gentle.[12] Not so the Germans. They must
be tough. They must steel themselves. They must show the Jews by
trampling with hob-nailed boots over their naked bodies.*

*There is another side to this "steel" business. You want to
steel yourself. I do not want to steel either myself or you. I am not
prepared to let you sharpen yourself on me. The only object I could
have in communicating with you would be to try to convert you, and
through you perhaps other Nazis. (I do not say Germans because
I still cling to the belief that those terms are not synonymous.) But
you are too sure of yourself to entertain the view which the whole
western world has of people like yourself.*

*In your present frame of mind you certainly ought not to come
to America, whether Canada or the United States. You will not be
welcome here. We do not want to teach you things which you can use
against us. Our greatest task—the task of the whole non-German
world, including Italy and probably Japan—is to make it impossible
for ideas such as those of the Nazis to prevail. It will not help us in
that task if we show our enemies how we do things.*

*If you really wanted to learn it would be different. But Nazism
conditions its people against learning. As likely as not you would
have the idea of verteidigen[13] Nazism here. For that there is no
room. We know what fine people the Germans are individually—
some of them, not the Prussian type—but we also know what their
failings are—their incapacity for self-government; their tendency
to submit to regimentation, which is repulsive to us; their inability
to attain co-operation without dictation; their utter lack of a normal
sense of humour.*

*It is not as if you were animated by missionary zeal like that of the
Christian missionaries. Your cult is not like that of the lowly Jew whom*

Luther served. You have abandoned the teaching of the 5th chapter of Matthew's Gospel. We don't make too good a job of it ourselves. But every Sunday our preachers of all denominations try to teach us mercy and love and humility—not force and steel and Gleichschaltung.

No, at best we would have to tolerate the Germans on the very principles of "love your enemies and pray for them which despitefully use you and persecute you."

This whole idea, of course, that a person of German blood (whatever that means) though resident, or perhaps born in, another country should somehow belong to the "Reich" of Germans is of course arrant nonsense to other nations. If a German is not satisfied in Germany he may go (or may he?) to Brazil; but then he is supposed to become a Brazilian. And to do that he is supposed to abjure his German citizenship. But the Germans don't want to play the game according to the rule. Once a German always a German. Says who? Says Germany. But we turn to the individual (who is not used to being consulted) and we say to him: What do you want? Do you want to become a Brazilian or a United Statesan? Or a British subject? If so, it is all right with us, but you must make up your mind. Now that is not the German idea. It is the race and not the individual that counts. The individual has no choice. The race claims him. But we say he is to be entirely free to choose his race (i.e. nationality)—for his children and even for himself. And this struggle is at the bottom of the whole question of policy. The Germans want Lebensraum. All right, we say, if there are too many people in Germany let them go to Canada or the United States or Czechoslovakia, or Rumania or wherever there is room. But at this the Germans let out an awful howl: "But they must remain German." Why must they remain German? Many people would say it was better for them in any case they should not remain German. Anyway, why should the rest of the world put itself out to make room for more Germans who want to be Germans? What about the Danes? There isn't room for all of them in Denmark. So they come to Canada and become good Canadians. What's wrong with that? Germans coming to Canada must be Anglicized as soon as possible and they should not congregate in German enclaves—in fact they do become good Anglicized citizens quickly and do not live in concentrated groups—excepting only rare cases.

It is ridiculous to say that the Frank who learned the Latin language is of different blood from the Frank on the other side of the Rhine who kept on speaking his rude Teutonic tongue.

It is an interesting problem in human relationships to figure out what, in the end, I ought to do about you (if indeed there is any "ought" about it). The fact that I knew you for only twenty minutes has nothing to do with the matter. Nor has the fact that I am two or three times as old as you. These are accidentals. The essentials are the motivations and sanctions behind or within you. If you have sold yourself to Nazism as Faust did to Mephistopheles, that is one thing. Or you may be a spy. Or you may be one of those, of whom there are many, who have taken on the task of reconciling people here, there and everywhere to Nazi ideas and practices. You may be one of those who wish (to use an Americanism) to sell Germany.... However the puzzle remains. What sort of a person are you? Is there any hope for you?

And so I spend these hours in trying to find a lodgment in your mind for these thoughts—not to replace the German things in it that are admirable, but to give you some chance to weigh and compare and estimate—if indeed there is room in the Nazi system for any such thing.

I am very much opposed to Chamberlain, but I would not murder him, nor he me. That is the generic difference between the Germans and British—I think we might also say between the Germans and the rest of the world.... So if you are that way—if you think what Hitler did to Roehm was the right thing to do—was a gentlemanly, decent menschlich,[14] how could there be any question, for example, of my being your guest? Can you answer me that?

GERMANS AND GERMANY IN 1938

5

The letters and diary of Franklin W. Wegenast offer a thoughtful contemporary look at Europe in early 1938, before the final slide into war, through the eyes of an outsider, a well-educated German Canadian, and a man who read such books as *Mein Kampf* and *Myth of the Twentieth Century*—works that formed the backbone of Nazi thinking. Newspaper reporting in Canada—whatever its deficiencies might be—had clearly given him enough information to know that he was visiting a troubled area, certainly troubled as far as the rest of the world was concerned. A review of the *Globe and Mail* reveals, however, that the voice of the German people somehow remained silent. What was it like to live under the Hitler regime and how did people feel about the situation? It was, of course, known at the time that Germans did not have the right to express themselves openly about either German conditions or about any potential deficiency of the Nazi party, but that made all the more tantalizing the issue of their opinions or even what a national opinion concerning such questions might be. These were difficult questions to answer in the 1930s, but they interested Wegenast.

He provided a particularly important commentary on German thinking, as well as life in Germany and the surrounding countries, because of his ability to speak various languages. He could communicate with everyday people. It is interesting to note that his success as a lawyer and his resulting social position in Canada did not disincline him to speak to ordinary people from all walks of life. And people seemed to respond to him, discussing rather openly and surprisingly how they felt about the situation. Because he was not a public figure, it was less dangerous to talk openly to him, and that fact probably made many converse with him more candidly than might otherwise have been the case. Frenchmen, Austrians, Germans, and Luxembourgers; farmers, truck drivers, barbers, doctors, ministers, and Mennonite Brethren told him how they saw the European situation, and what they made of

Hitlerism. He focused on talking to people in the countryside. Wegenast wrote remarkably little about the large European cities that he visited: he believed that all major cities shared common characteristics, and characteristics that undermined the distinctive culture of a nation. If one wanted to know how Germans or Frenchmen thought, one should talk to those living in small villages or on farms, it seemed to him.

Wegenast offered rather interesting ideas on how Nazism sustained popularity. For one thing, he believed that support rested on an ability to avoid thinking about aspects of Hitlerism that were unacceptable to western democracies. In Wegenast's discussions with Germans, he often noted their intense concern, usually seen in consort with support of Hitlerism, with what the rest of the world thought of them. Virtually every German he talked to asked him what opinions were held in the Ausland of Germany. Not only that, but any sign he made of appreciation of German things—hotels, for example—met with pleased responses because it meant appreciation of what Germany stood for. This suggested to the Canadian visitor that Germans knew that their general philosophy was unacceptable to others, and that therefore they were conscious that they were playing a dangerous game. Germans were fully aware of the murky path they had set out for themselves, Wegenast believed, and also recognized to what extent many outside Germany feared and despised them because of Hitlerism. "No one likes me, so I'll go in the garden and eat worms," was the way he put it. This obsession with what the world thought, observed by Wegenast, was evidenced in the extreme reactions of Hitler to comments made by people in the American press—LaGuardia, for example, and Dodd. The overwhelming concern with the views of other nations means something else—Germans were more aware of the terrible things that were going on in Germany than they often later admitted, and didn't want to think about it.

Wegenast also believed a significant number of individuals exuded lethargy, and often angry lethargy at that, over the situation. He interpreted this feeling as evidence of passive (but often hidden) resistance to certain Nazi policies. Most people outside Germany in adjacent countries (certainly all non-ethnic Germans) that Wegenast spoke with shared his general anti-Nazi point of view. He realized, however, that it could often be hard for visitors in areas adjoining Germany to accept that idea. For example, the Reich regularly sent Germans into Austria to lead rallies or march in parades. Under these conditions, a press reporter (especially a foreign reporter) would find it difficult to discern who was a national German and who was a national Austrian. The movement of school children across borders both ways was part of the same pattern. In spite of suspecting an underlying lethargy,

Wegenast was prepared to admit the mesmerizing effects that Hitler had on crowds when he spoke at rallies. Other visitors in the 1930s saw the same thing and puzzled over the ultimate meaning of the animal magnetism behind Hitler's speeches. For example, the Swiss intellectual Denis de Rougemont, after hearing a rally in the spring of 1936, wrote: "Has Hitler hypnotized his nation, now prey to the nightmare of force, with the cry of *Germany awake!?* Or is it that the truth of this nation has become apparent today and that we were the ones dreaming when we thought it had charms?"[1]

The dichotomy of angry lethargy when combined with hysteria over Hitler speeches was one aspect of what Wegenast saw as irrationality behind German thinking. At its core, he believed support of Nazism itself rested on irrationality. Take the German attitude to war, for example. Wegenast could see that Germans actively did not want war, yet they supported activities that could only ultimately bring war. He concluded that this approach was based on the German belief that Hitler could follow such dangerous paths and get what he wanted without war. Wegenast found it impossible to reconcile the two thoughts with each other in any rational way, however. Such an approach seemed to him a form of irrationality. Striving for economic growth at the expense of personal freedom also struck Wegenast as an illogical (and therefore irrational) aspect of German thinking, and as a fundamental rejection of civilized living. Nazism might be viewed an economic and political machine, but its subversive side-effects, such as imprisoning people with no semblance of a trial, were shrugged off by virtually all Germans that Wegenast talked to. Personal freedom seemed immaterial to them, something that was incomprehensible to the Canadian lawyer trained in British law.

Racial hate and obsession with race he found fundamental to not just Nazism but also to the thinking of individual Germans who believed in Hitler. Wegenast bought Rosenberg's *The Myth of the Twentieth Century* and made notes on the book—trying to make sense of the racial statements contained in it. The race issues inherent in Nazism and Rosenberg's work seemed to Wegenast to seethe beneath the surface of German thinking, and while not openly evident, anti-Semitism was always just below the surface. It could erupt at any time and did so when Wegenast talked to people, even his relatives. He did not pull punches when such topics came up, never hesitating to point out how irrational such thinking was. He tried hard not to let his opinions on such matters interfere with how he felt about individuals personally, and he informed people to that effect. Wegenast also read the French version of *Mein Kampf*. People who spoke only English would not be able to read what Hitler originally wrote until just before the outbreak of war, a situation that hindered an understanding of the true depths of the dangers inherent in Nazism.[2]

The presence of the First World War could be found everywhere in Europe—from the remains of trenches to national cemeteries and ruined churches. Wegenast discussed the war with Frenchmen in a comradely way, but tried not to be drawn into any talk concerning the war while in Germany. He was well aware of the obsession with the Treaty of Versailles, which he did not believe to be the cause of the German militarism of the 1930s. The tendency to blame the treaty for the world situation and developments in Germany, prevalent in many circles (including the British press), angered Wegenast. He was particularly annoyed with Germans who, he stated, wanted to fight the war all over again. It was difficult for anyone Wegenast's age to forget the fact that Germany had been a fearsome enemy. Had nothing been solved? Did it really have to happen again? Had Germany become even more German?

His observations about life in Germany could be particularly acute, especially in light of contemporary views. Visitors often commented, for example, on the positive effect Hitler had had on the economy, George Drew being an example. Wegenast had this to say about the German economy and Hitler's importance to its growth, based on his double observations of certain areas in both 1921 and 1938: "Nazism and Hitlerism are the result, and not the cause of revival in Germany. The enormous headway which Germany is making was on the way before Hitler ever came on the scene.... The Germans are kidding the world and themselves into thinking it is Hitler that has ushered in the era of prosperity. Bunk."[3]

Wegenast remarked on other aspects of life in Nazi Germany. He felt the social power of the Nazi Party everywhere. Members were in effect the social elite, the ruling class. He sensed, in contrast, a reduction of the presence of Prussian aristocratic militarism. The presence of the military and militarism on a more de-classed level, however, was everywhere. One saw soldiers in all areas. He commented on the efficiency and cleanliness of all aspects of public life in Germany compared to France where he encountered both dirty hotels and unclean cathedrals. Wegenast took a great deal of interest in the position of women in Germany. He believed their ability to function in professions and business had been severely restricted. It seemed to Wegenast that the chief role of women in Germany, according to the state, was to produce more Germans and German soldiers at that. He noticed that few were members of the Nazi party. He entertained no sympathy for this general degradation of women. Wegenast saw a lot of style in the dressing of German women, and believed they matched French women in that capacity.

The atmosphere in Germany influenced attitudes to Nazism, Wegenast found. Members of the German Nafziger family who lived in Luxembourg did not think much of Nazi policy, while at least one member of this family who lived in Germany was a rabid supporter of Hitler. Even within the Wegenast family, members within Germany seemed to have a greater tendency to favour Hitler and Nazi racist thought than those living outside Germany; witness the opinions of family members in Heidelberg versus those of family members living in Trieste. Surviving collections of contemporary correspondence corroborate this pattern. One young German woman living in the Netherlands, for example, wrote home to her mother about the atrocious things she had heard that were happening to Jews in Germany in the 1930s. The mother informed her daughter that the Jews had to be dealt with.[4] A German citizen in Germany could feel differently, apparently, about racial issues than a German citizen who lived elsewhere.

His commentary reveals that he was not above common North American biases of the time. When one first reads this diary it is easy to shudder at what is not politically acceptable today—a discussion of heinies or frogs or wops. His philosophizing showed that he himself did not associate such terms with derogatory characteristics. He did not appear to use the word heinie, for example, in a particularly hateful way. Some of Wegenast's strongest biased statements arose from his pro-British stance. It is clear that he had absorbed some of his convictions concerning British characteristics from material that he read. It was a German writer, Stoye, who supported the idea that what defined an Englishman was his gentlemanliness.[5] The point of view fit with Wegenast's own experiences, so he adopted it. Others seemed to read through the compliment, believing that Stoye's statements were intended to woo Britain for support, something that Wegenast did not appear to perceive. His interest in people, and evidence that he could relate freely with people of many classes in many nations denied a certain narrowness of opinion that normally accompanied such biases.

It was the letters between Sigfrid Schmidt and Wegenast, with their commentary on the question of race, that reveal how much the Canadian visitor wanted to make sense of the heartbeat of Nazism. It is interesting to note in passing that when he met Schmidt in Reims, it appeared to Wegenast that Schmidt was not a supporter of Nazi philosophy. The correspondence revealed otherwise.[6] When Wegenast began writing to Sigfrid Schmidt, he could marshal his thoughts well because he had worked out his ideas in the diary, especially concerning Rosenberg's contentions. Wegenast also contextualized his remarks about German sentiments historically. The Sigfrid Schmidt file, that is the Schmidt/Wegenast correspondence (and abortive correspondence), is filled with discussions relating to the complicated subject of the role of myth in history, the veracity of history, the veracity of myth within history, and the relation of both or either to social conditions of the time. Historic myth making lay behind Rosenberg's words, and Sigfrid's absorption of them showed how a German could synthesize them into something seemingly rational. Sigfrid used history—German and British—to verify his "Germanness," and his interpretation of history was clearly steeped in myth, especially Romantic nineteenth century *Völkisch* myth. Wegenast's attempt to separate myth making from historical thinking was at the root of his arguments, albeit somewhat unconsciously, and at the root of his attempt to show the irrationality of Sigfrid's position. It seems clear, however, that Wegenast was also influenced by myth himself, even if he thought he was expressing factual "history." The idea of Scottish parliament that existed 1000 years ago had been debunked as being merely myth by the time he was writing about it to Sigfrid. It was evident that the idea of an ancient Scottish parliament was invented in the 16th century by James Buchanan, a brilliant humanist, to support the disposition of Mary Queen of Scots.[7]

The racism inherent in Sigfrid's words seemed to compound his existing disgust with the incipient eugenics he had found in Rosenberg's writings, racial purity issues that formed Nazi thought, and the sexism he had observed in Germany. The diary indicated that Wegenast had demonstrated no sympathy for the eugenic racism, or ethnic breeding ideology that he encountered in Germany and that he abhorred the treatment of women and their degradation as breeding machines. It would appear too that he had never entertained eugenic views while in Canada. The birth control issue had been simply a legal issue over women's right to control their bodies. How much respect he maintained after the German experience for active eugenicists in North America is another question. No documentation exists to answer the question.

While scholarship and the surfacing of primary documentation over the last number of years has allowed for the gathering of information on the nature of German thinking in a way that was not possible in the 1930s, the questions that Wegenast addressed remain difficult to answer fully even today, as Kershaw recently pointed out.[8] Wegenast's observations add to the compilation of material that can be useful in a study of these problems. While his views are only that of one individual, they were acute and relate easily to the general consensus of historians. Certain important perceptions of Wegenast's fit well with the modern scholarship found in the recent writing of such historians as I. Kershaw, R. Evans, R. Bessel, P. Fritzsche, R. Gellately, and C. Koonz, whose works are listed in the bibliography. All contend, for example, that regardless of the repression of ideas in Germany, the vast majority of Germans did not want Hitler removed. Repression did not fully explain the silence evident in press reports. Most scholars suggest, though, that a sullen lethargy griped the people. Incipient racism and anti-Semitism, all would argue, played a role in German acceptance of the Hitler regime, even though some of these historians would point out that other issues had significant roles in that acceptance.

Most scholars would also side with Wegenast on his views concerning Hitler and the German economy. The opinions held by Lloyd George and others of similar mind set, including Germans in the 1930s, concerning the nature of Hitler's effects on the German economy, are today considered to be incorrect. First, signs of economic recovery existed before Hitler came to power; and second, the economy was not as robust under Hitler as many at the time claimed it to be.[9]

All scholars agree that, regardless of the validity of the point of view, the Treaty of Versailles played a major role in shaping German attitudes to international affairs. Here Wegenast deviated somewhat from the prevailing modern scholarly point of view. His support for the treaty seemed to blind him to the reality that its emotional significance for Germans had been huge. He was aware of German reactions to the treaty, and he knew that many people in Britain agreed with the basic German point of view. But Wegenast was not prepared to reject the view that Germany got what it deserved at the end of the First World War. Historians argue that, regardless of its validity or fairness, many Germans took the treaty to mean that the country faced implacable enemies on all sides. Germany had suffered a near death in 1918, and Hitler has rescued the nation. Because Germans suspected that hate was directed at them, they in turn learned to hate and subsequently to see enemies where none existed previous to the advent of Hitler. Wegenast's observations concerning German obsession with world estimation of them and Germany, however, fit into a prevailing general fixation with foreign opinion that had been in place for some time.

P. Fritzsche wrote in 2008, "The violence of the Nazis was so excessive and their feeling of liberation from conventional morality so complete that any attempt at explanation falters,"[10] except perhaps that hate ringed them. The situation reinforced the need to see national affairs in racial terms. The business of race came to define how Germans saw the world. It was to what extent ordinary Germans accepted the idea of racial superiority, this scholar added, that made them become Nazis in the years 1933–1945. Fritzsche stated the following:

> In many ways, the political success of Nazism rested on whether individual Germans came to see the world through the lenses of racial comradeship and racial struggle.... Indeed, with the concept

of race, National Socialists dramatized each of the elements in the equation of national renewal. Once radicalized, dangers appeared to be more frightening, while solutions become more drastic and the mobilization they required more complex, and more likely to end in war. For the Nazis, race worked as an exponential power.[11]

Wegenast's views also often echoed those of individuals who lived in Germany under Hitler. Victor Klemperer, a German Jew, survived the entire Hitler period within Germany and kept a lengthy diary from 1933 until 1945. (The document was not published until the late 1990s, long after Klemperer's death.) A few passages from Klemperer's diary, written in 1936 and 1937, are worth quoting, because they reveal the startling similarity of the two men's points of view on certain issues: general acceptance of Hitler along with lethargy, fear of outsiders, a strong sense of racism, and a feeling of helplessness. On May 16, 1936, Klemperer wrote:

I certainly no longer believe that [the German Government] has enemies inside Germany. The majority of the people are content, a small group accepts Hitler as the lesser evil, no one really wants to get rid of him, all see in him the liberator of foreign affairs, fear Russian conditions, as a child fears the bogeyman, believe insofar as they are not honestly carried away, that it is inopportune, in terms of Realpolitik, to be outraged at such details as the suppression of civil liberties, the persecution of the Jews, the falsification of all scholarly truth, the systematic destruction of all morality. And all are afraid for their livelihood, their life, all are such terrible cowards. (Can I reproach them for it? During my last year in my post [as a university professor] I swore an oath to Hitler, I have remained in the country—I am no better than my Aryan fellow creatures.)[12]

On March 27, 1937, he noted "There is so much lethargy in the German people and so much immorality and above all this so much stupidity."[13] By June of that year, he had begun to analyze the nature of this German lethargy.

The never ending alarms, the never ending phrases, the never ending hanging out of flags, now in triumph, now in mourning—it all produces apathy. And everyone feels helpless, and everyone knows he is lied to, and everyone is told what he has to believe. Whether one gets a quarter pound of butter tomorrow or not, is much more important than all the problems with Spain and the Vatican. And probably no one expects war anymore; people have gotten used to the foreign powers putting up with everything.[14]

Klemperer saw himself as a German and Germany as his fatherland. For some time he could not bring himself to believe that Hitler spoke for the majority of Germans. By summer of 1937 he had changed his mind. On July 13 of that year, he stated: "I said to myself once again, that Hitlerism is after all more deeply and firmly rooted in the nation and corresponds more to the German nature than I would like to admit."[15] The following month he elaborated on this theme:

The Claim of the NSDAP to express the true opinion of the German people [seems more and more to be correct]. And I believe ever more strongly that Hitler really does embody the soul of the German people, that he really stands for "Germany" and that he will consequently maintain himself and justifiably maintain himself. Whereby I have not only outwardly lost my Fatherland. And even if the government should change one day: my inner sense of belonging is gone.[16]

It is interesting that the novelist Irène Némirovsky, who lived in France until she was killed at Auschwitz in 1942, spoke of French public opinion in her book *All Our Worldly Goods* in much the same way when it came to a general sense of lethargy, and the relationship of Hitler's entrenchment to a sense of impending doom. "Everyone waited for the war to start the way people wait for death: knowing it is inevitable, asking only for a little more time," she wrote. "So, in 1938, people sensed the constant presence of war, invisible yet all around them. Death took them by the hand and led them where it pleased; it made their food horribly bitter, poisoned their pleasures; death stood at their side as they leaned over the cradles of newborn children."[17]

Wegenast expended a great deal of energy trying to understand what in the end he found incomprehensible. While he had seen German developments before early 1938 as a road to madness, he had entertained a faint hope that reason ultimately could be made to prevail and thus war averted. His letters to several Germans revealed the endurance of that faith. In the draft papers he composed for Sigfrid Schmidt, he tried to show how different Germany's philosophical base was from that in other countries. His thoughts became repetitive and obsessive, perhaps showing his deepening sense of helplessness. It is possible that increasing ill health also sapped his energy. By late 1938, he no longer entertained any hope for a change of heart in Germans or for peace. There was no turning of a tide of irrationality, evil as it was. The road to war was built, and, in his opinion, it was paved on racial hate. Nothing could reverse that situation now. In the end Wegenast came to believe that he had to repudiate a lot of what he himself was—his German background, heritage, and, to some degree, his relatives—when he concluded that Germany would take the world to war. The resulting pressure from these thoughts must have further drained his energy.

There was a shift in tenor in the *Globe and Mail* by late 1938, which matched the hardening of Wegenast's sense of hopelessness. The ricocheting fear and concurrent sensationalism about the real possibility of war, evident in the paper over 1937 and early 1938, was replaced increasingly by the end of 1938 with an acceptance of the idea that confrontation was unavoidable. The Kristallnacht pogrom against Jews in the late fall of 1938 escalated the sense of horror concerning Nazi Germany in Europe and North America. Germany's actions were unacceptable, and the future for the western world looked bleak as a result. The paper commented in the following way, for example, on the increasingly virulent and incomprehensible anti-Semitism in Germany. "By the anti-Jewish measures taken by Germany and the brutality of the attack on the persons and properties of Jews that any agreement signed by the Reich government is apt to be considered as a mere scrap of paper intended to conceal other designs," *Globe and Mail* stated in December 1938.[18] In late 1938 Hitler openly threatened to use force to stop any country speaking out against Germany, a situation that did not lead to conciliatory feelings toward Germany.[19] Germany's takeover of Czechoslovakia made international relations even more difficult.

In December of 1938 a series of articles in the *Globe and Mail* provided information on life in Germany, more particularly Berlin, in detail not seen before in the Canadian paper. They were written by Harold Callender, a staff correspondent for the *New York Times*, and sent from Paris. Callender attempted in his reviews to penetrate the nature of German attitudes, and focused on the virulent and rising strength of anti-Semitism that accompanied the aftermath of the Kristallnacht pogrom. Callender spoke of witnessing what "the solution to the Jewish problem has meant so far in terms of human casualties and suffering.... It is difficult to believe that such a catastrophe could have been the deliberate systematic work of any human will." Jews are the chief sufferers but by no means the only ones, Callender argued. He also believed that many Germans did not support such activities because they had been taken too far. The point that Callender wanted to make, though, above and beyond exposing the existing horror, was that it no longer mattered what Germans thought. Their opinions would have no effect on future activities of the German nation.

Callender could not believe that no serious opposition to Hitler existed in Germany, even if such opposition remained hidden. "All over Germany and even in the Nazi ranks there are many who are shocked and shamed by what has been done in the name of the German people. They bitterly resent the official assertion that the onslaught on the Jews was a spontaneous act of the German nation—an assertion they consider a slander upon Germany. But what the Germans generally think is largely immaterial for few dare to give much help to Jews and none dares openly to criticize." Even mild expressions of criticism resulted in imprisonment, he noted, but allowed that in the privacy of their homes many Germans condemned the activities. Jews knew that they had no future in Germany, and many educated men felt lucky to escape with their lives. With many men in concentration camps, leaving their families to fend for themselves, it was hard to make sense of this brutality, Callender said. He presented theories, one financial, but a second that arose from the view that "the main purpose is to intimidate opponents of the Nazis at home and abroad by a show of ruthlessness."[20] There is much evidence to counter Callender's view that Germans feared Hitler's path; certainly Wegenast's impressions were otherwise, although it is true that the situation had changed hugely between the time Wegenast visited Germany and the time that Callender was writing about. While Callender saw repression and fear in Berlin, Wegenast had seen exhilaration in southwest Germany, based on an intensified sense of being German from deeply embedded cultural tenets. Both points of view suggested that war was inevitable, but they did so for differing reasons, indicating the complexity of German thinking.

Canadian readers reacted to Callender's words, expressing opinions of those outside Germany. One wrote in to say: "To ordinary God-fearing people there are no standards by which to judge such savagery.... Mad power, the whole system has been built on hate.... There is no pretending that there can be peace with such ruthless blackguards. Force is their creed, and force alone will bring them down."[21] A few days later, Callender sent in another report that reinforced his earlier statements but also showed evidence of conflicting views and dichotomous statements about the state of German thinking. The *Globe and Mail* reported what Callender had to say: It no longer mattered what Germans as a people thought, Callender began. "In Germany today one finds a curious mixture of feelings and views that may perhaps be summed up as a consciousness of tremendous power, subjected to scarcely any immediate restraints at home or abroad, that seems to be moving swiftly toward ends which no one can be certain and of which the best informed are keenly apprehensive.... It is difficult to gauge German public opinion, for it is not supposed to exist, insomuch as all Germans are officially regarded as backing Chancellor Hitler as one man. It is believed that telephones are tapped by the secret police, letters opened and suspected dissenters closely watched." Spies are everywhere and thinking Germans only speak in low whispers to each other, Callender added and he offered the following thoughts, "Yet one finds plenty of evidence in all classes of acute apprehension as to where the country is being led, and hope is repeatedly expressed that foreign powers will yet check Nazi 'dynamism.'" He went on to say that Germans claimed that there was nothing they could do—the power of the state was too strong. Germans had hated the idea of war over the Sudetenland issue, and only cheered when the annexation was achieved without war. Many Germans believed that that would not be possible for much longer and that is one reason they feared the future with Hitler in charge—they feared he would not stop. Some Germans had wanted war over Sudetenland because Germany would have been crushed and Hitler removed, Callender concluded.[22] While Callender and others clearly could make no more sense of the race-driven programs of Hitler than could Wegenast, the Sigfrid Schmidt letters provide a very different point of view concerning German support of Hitler in the deepening crisis. Wegenast believed that Germans in general continued to support Hitlerism and its contingent racism.

There seems to be little question, from the evidence of modern scholarship, including various types of sources and contemporary diaries, that Callender painted an overly optimistic picture of resistance by Germans in Germany to Nazism. Wegenast's views conform better with the modern general consensus: the vast majority of German people supported Hitler and his regime enough to prevent any real opposition to either. Wegenast also grasped the complex and often contradictory nature of Hitler's leadership that puzzled so many contemporaries in countries outside Germany, and seemed to puzzle Callender as well. Hitler was not a dictator as far as Germans were concerned. They did not bow to Hitler so much as believe that he shared their point of view. He gave them what they wanted.[23] As Sigfrid Schmidt told Wegenast, "We serve [Hitler] because he is himself our first servant; we follow him because we love him," and added "We Germans do not want war."[24]

This personal evaluation of Hitler and Germany serves to remind us of something that is critical when assessing contemporary points of view on any subject: namely what is obvious today might not have been so obvious to those living through the times. Because we understand the situation in Germany in the late 1930s much better than even ten years ago—let alone at the time events took place—it is often all too tempting to see Wegenast's agonized efforts to make sense of Germany simply as wasted energy over the obvious, for example his repeated strong condemnation of Hitler and the Nazi party, or his conclusion that race obsession (not economic issues) explained the heartbeat of Nazism. When reading what he wrote, it is important to remember that he saw the situation within the framework of his time, and he could not know what we know as a result of modern scholarship, contemporary material produced within Germany and now available, and perhaps most significantly, with the advantage of hindsight.

NOTES

Notes to Introduction

1 The birth control trial of 1936, also known as the Dorothea Palmer trial, arose over the issue of the selling of contraceptives by the Parents' Information Bureau, an organization set up by A.R. Kaufman in 1930. Selling contraceptives was against the Criminal Code. Wegenast won the case on the basis that the distribution of contraceptives was in the interest of the public good. The private papers of F.W. Wegenast contain information on the trial. See as well Augustine, Ham, Kaufman family fonds, [1877?]–1990, Archives, University of Waterloo Library; Margaret Hyndman Tapes, Ontario Archives, July 1983; A. McLaren, *Our Master Race: Eugenics in Canada, 1885–1945*, Toronto: McClelland and Stewart, 1990; and Parents' Information Bureau fonds, 1930–1976, Archives, University of Waterloo Library.

2 See, for example, "Stability and Change," *Times*, August 4, 1937, 13; "Anglo-German Relations. Abandoning the 'Anti' Attitude," August 11, 1937, 8. See also F.R. Gannon, *The British Press and Germany, 1936–1939* (Oxford: Clarendon Press, 1971), 2, 3, 10–11, 15–16, 69–74.

3 Col. George A. Drew, "Finds Germany Touches Peak of Efficiency," *Globe and Mail*, August 16, 1937, 1, 3.

4 Victor Klemperer, *I Will Bear Witness, 1933–1941: A Diary of the Nazi Years*, volume 1, translated by Martin Chalmers (New York: Modern Library, 1999).

5 Lloyd George, "I Talked to Hitler," *Daily Express*, November 17, 1936. Quoted in *The Nazi Years: A Documentary History,* ed., J. Remak (Englewood Cliffs: Prentice-Hall, 1969), 81–82.

6 William Lyon Mackenzie King, *The Diaries of William Lyon Mackenzie King*, June 29, 1937, 630, 632. Online http://www.collectionscanada.gc.ca/databases/king/index-e.html.

7 Klemperer, *I Will Bear Witness.*

8 See, for example, I. Kershaw's *Hitler* (London: Allan Lane, 2008), and his *Hitler, the Germans, and the Final Solution* (New Haven: Yale University Press, 2008), as well as his *The Nazi Dictatorship: Problems and Perspectives of Interpretation,* fourth edition (London: Arnold, 2000). See also R.J. Evans's *The Third Reich in Power, 1933–1939* (New York: Penguin Press, 2005).

9 O. Lubrich, ed., *Travels in the Reich, 1933–1945: Foreign Authors Report from Germany.* Translated by Kenneth Northcott, Sonia Wichmann, and Dean Krouk (Chicago: University of Chicago Press, 2010), 2.

10 A. Rosenberg, *Myth of the Twentieth Century* (1930); reissued by Noontide Press, Newport Beach, CA, 1982. Online in English: http://www.archive.org/details/TheMythOfThe20thCentury. In German, *Der Mythus des XX. Jahrhunderts* online: http://www.archive.org/details/DerMythusDes20Jahrhunderts.

Notes to Chapter 1

1 G. Leibbrandt, *Little Paradise: The Saga of the German Canadians of Waterloo, 1800–1975* (Kitchener, ON: Allprint, 1980) 71, 89, 92, 94, 132, 134.

2 Information on the life of Franklin Wellington Wegenast comes from the Wegenast Family Papers, Private Collection.

3 Information on Margaret Mary Bell comes from the Margaret Bell Family Papers, Private Collection.

4 The A.T.C.M. Associate degree was the highest level of accreditation from the Toronto Conservatory of Music between 1896 and 1947.

5 John Soper McKay was called to the bar in 1883.

6 Osgoode Hall was the only accredited law school in Ontario between 1889 and 1957. In order to practise law one had to pass examinations at Osgoode, set by the Law Society. The L.L.B., Bachelor of Laws, was an undergraduate degree in law and did not qualify a person to practise law. Education for the law at the beginning of the 20th century was varied and complicated. The L.L.B. held more prestige than a high school degree. One could article with only a grammar school education and then sit for the bar exams.

7 Sir William Meredith was leader of the Ontario Conservatives from 1878 until 1894. He was Chief Justice of Ontario from 1912 to 1923. Meredith articled for two years after completing grammar school. He was called to the bar in 1861, and received an L.L.B. from the University of Toronto in 1872. He was elected a Bencher of the Law Society of Ontario in 1871.

8 Wegenast to his wife, continuous journal November 1920, Wegenast Family Papers, Private Collection.

9 A short diary of this trip survived. Wegenast Family Papers, Private Collection.

10 The book, well known to lawyers over a long period of time, is F.W. Wegenast, *The Law of Canadian Companies* (Toronto: Burroughs and Company, 1931).

11 For more on Margaret Hyndman, see M. Porter, "The Legal Lady," *Maclean's Magazine*, July 15, 1949, 15, 22–24.

12 Margaret Hyndman wrote the preface of the 1980 reissued edition of his book, and spoke of these pursuits.

13 His research material on the subject, and a few published articles exist in the Wegenast Family Papers, Private Collection.

14 See Augustine, Ham, Kaufman Family Fonds, [1877?]–1990. Archives, University of Waterloo.

15 Dorothea Palmer Collection, Archives, University of Waterloo.

16 Dorothea Palmer Collection.

17 Margaret Hyndman Tapes, Ontario Archives, 1983. The files of the Dorothea Palmer Collection, interestingly, contain nothing by Margaret Hyndman concerning the argument. Some of the papers setting out legal precedent are not in his writing and might be hers—but from one short note in her handwriting it doesn't look like it.

18 Margaret Hyndman Tapes; A. McLaren, *Our Master Race: Eugenics in Canada, 1885–1945* (Toronto: McClelland and Stewart, 1990), 84.
19 See the Parent's Information Bureau Fonds, Archives, University of Waterloo.
20 McLaren, *Our Master Race*, 115–16.
21 Ibid., 116.
22 Ibid., 115–16.
23 Ibid., 84–85.
24 Ibid., 85–86.
25 This overview of issues at the trial has been drawn from various files in the Dorothea Palmer Collection, Archives, University of Waterloo. The collection is very large, but includes several copies of many of the documents.

Notes to Chapter 2
1 See F.R. Gannon, *The British Press and Germany, 1936–1939* (Oxford: Clarendon Press, 1971), 2, 3, 5, 10–11, 15–16, 69–74.
2 "Stability and Change," *Times*, August 4, 1937, 13.
3 George Shee, "Anglo-German Relations. Abandoning the 'Anti' Attitude," *Times*, August 11, 1937, 8.
4 "Empire Is World's Hope," *Globe*, November 6, 1936, 4, 15.
5 Johannes Stoye, translated by W. Payne, *The British Empire: Its Structure and Its Problems* (London: John Lane, 1936).
6 "Empire Inspires Respect," *Globe and Mail*, December 11, 1936, 6.
7 "German Lauds British Empire in Analysis of Its Character," *Globe and Mail*, December 19, 1936, 10.
8 "Move Forced by Gentiles, States Club," *Globe and Mail*, June 22, 1937, 4.
9 "Britain Endorses Jewish and Arab Separate States," *Globe and Mail*, July 8, 1937, 1; "Britain's Palestine Plan," *Globe and Mail*, July 8, 1937, 6.
10 "Lurid Sign Warns Jews off East End Beach," *Globe and Mail*, August 3, 1937, 4.
11 "Anti-Semitism Held Growing in England," *Globe*, November 5, 1936, 13.
12 "Law Winks at English Fascists," *Globe and Mail*, January 21, 1938, 6.
13 "German Jews Lose Status," *Globe and Mail*, June 15, 1937, 10.
14 "Jew-Baiter Asks Death as Penalty," *Globe and Mail*, June 22, 1937, 1.
15 "Rotary Clubs Banned in Germany as Anti-Nazi," *Globe and Mail*, August 25, 1937, 1, 3.
16 "Nazis Renew War on Jews and Catholics," *Globe and Mail*, January 4, 1938, 1.
17 "Tolerance of the Majority," *Globe and Mail*, June 30, 1937, 6.
18 "London on Alert for Large Scale Military Thrust," *Globe and Mail*, December 24, 1936, 1.
19 "What Next, Hitler?" *Globe and Mail*, December 25, 1936, 6.
20 "Nazi Demands Are Prepared; War Talk Gains: Press Is Pessimistic; Rejection Is Seen," *Globe and Mail*, February 2, 1937, 1.
21 "No War Danger, Goebbels Says," *Globe and Mail*, February 13, 1937, 1.
22 "Nazi Press in Fury at New York Mayor for Gibe at Hitler," *Globe and Mail*, March 5, 1937, 1.
23 Ibid., 1–3.
24 "La Guardia, Scorning U.S. Apology, Again Slaps Hitler," *Globe and Mail*, March 6, 1937, 1.

25 "Nazi Press Denounced by U.S. Ambassador for Course Comment," *Globe and Mail*, March 13, 1937, 1.

26 "New York Throng Hears Hitler Flayed as 'Cruelly Vile,'" *Globe and Mail*, March 16, 1937, 1, 2.

27 "Mayor La Guardia Again in Nazi Hair," *Globe and Mail*, March 17, 1937, 1, 3; King noted Göring's dislike of Americans. Baron von Neurath explained to King that the dislike many Germans had for Americans stemmed from the remarks that La Guardia had made about Hitler. *The Diaries of William Lyon Mackenzie King*, July 30, 1937, 636–37.

28 Ibid.

29 "Hitler Warned by Britain and France"; "Germany Demands Free Hand"; "Hope to Stall until Nations' Tempers Cool"; "Told to Go Easy Lest He Plunge Europe into War," *Globe and Mail*, June 1, 1937, 1.

30 "Reich Won't Start War, Says Hitler, but Ready to Strike if Attacked," *Globe and Mail*, June 7, 1937, 1, 3.

31 "The New European Calm," *Globe and Mail*, June 15, 1937, 6.

32 "Leaders of Church Defy Nazis," *Globe and Mail*, July 26, 1937, 1.

33 "Nazi Effort Being Made to Drop Trial," *Globe and Mail*, August 10, 1937, 1. See *The Times* as well, including "Nazi Police and the Church," *Times*, August 3, 1937, 9; "German Protestant Defiance; Another Church Leader Detained," *Times*, August 10, 1937, 6.

34 "Niemoeller Is Refused Public Trial," *Globe and Mail*, February 8, 1938, 13.

35 "Niemoeller, Defiant, Fires Three Lawyers, Directs Own Defense," *Globe and Mail*, February 9, 1938, 1.

36 "Nazi Chief Eases Gag on Church," *Globe and Mail*, February 19, 1938, 2.

37 R.J. Evans, *The Third Reich in Power* (New York: Penguin Books, 2005), 220–33.

38 Evans, *Third Reich in Power*, 646–59.

39 A difficult word to translate, because no single word, or even set of phrases, carries all its meanings and implications. Wegenast uses the word under different contexts in the diary. In most literal terms it means systematic smashing, or taming. Coordination of all independent agencies or organizations. A policy initiated by Hitler in 1933 with the destruction of historic rights of separate states of Germany, dismissal of their governments and appointment of Reich governors. By July 1933 Hitler's Party was the only legal party. Gleichschaltung extended to the press. A law in October 1933 ordered that all newspaper editors be German citizens, Aryan by race, and not married to Jews. Censorship laws in relation to education were also part of Gleichschaltung.

40 Means union, inclusion, attachment to, or annexation of. The Anschluss was planned in 1937—the acquisition of first Austria and then Czechoslovakia.

41 Nazi Coup in Austria Hits Snag, *Globe and Mail*, February 17, 1938, 1, 2.

42 Ibid.

43 "Hitler Slays a Wicked Tyrant," *Globe and Mail*, February 17, 1938, 13.

44 "Resistance at Vienna Is Crushed," *Globe and Mail*, February 18, 1938, 1; "London Studies Implications of Nazi Coup," *Globe and Mail*, February 18, 1938, 3.

45 World view, philosophy of a world outlook. World perception of a person, group, a people—shapes views, creates political boundaries.

46 "German Nazis Barred from Interfering in Vienna's Affairs," *Globe and Mail*, February 19, 1938, 1.

47 "German Nazis Keep Hands Off," *Globe and Mail*, February 19, 1938, 2.

48 Ibid.

49 "Will Not Permit Any Interference in Plans, He Says," *Globe and Mail*, February 21, 1938, 1, 2.

50 "Vienna Hears Nazis' Shouts of 'Heil Hitler,'" *Globe and Mail*, February 21, 1938, 48.

51 "Drang Nach Osten" means "thrust to the east," a push east at the expense of the Slavs (especially in Czechoslovakia), to fill the need for more living space for Germans (lebensraum).

52 "Will Not Permit Any Interference in Plans, He Says," *Globe and Mail*, February 21, 1938, 1, 2; "Hitler Heralds Wider Mid-European Sway," *Globe and Mail*, February 21, 1938, 2.

53 "Hitler Heralds Wider Mid-European Sway," *Globe and Mail*, February 21, 1938, 2.

54 "Nazi Parade Routed by Vienna Police," *Globe and Mail*, February 22, 1938, 13.

55 "Police at Loss When Jewish Dentist Slain," *Globe and Mail*, February 22, 1938, 13.

56 "Fear of Nazis Grips Austria, Jews Suicide," *Globe and Mail*, February 23, 1938, 12.

57 "Czechs Are Prepared to Ward Off Attacks Alone, Says General," *Globe and Mail*, February 24, 1938, 1.

58 "Schushnigg's Defiance Inflames Nazis; Hitler Lashes Provocateurs Who Stir Hate," *Globe and Mail*, February 25, 1938, 1.

59 By late 1938 and early 1939, after Wegenast had returned home, the situation for Jews in Europe had worsened considerably, and the *Globe and Mail* reported on conditions in detail, with a stronger focus on race. See the paper for "Nazis May Force Jews to Aid German Exports," December 13, 1938, 2; "Reich Sets Trade Price for Jew Aid," December 17, 1938, 1; "'Blackmail' Seen in Nazi Plan for Jews," December 19, 1938, 1; "International Terror and Intimidation Seen in Nazi War on Jews," December 19, 1938, 3; "Work at Peace with Majority, Jews Warned," December 19, 1938, 5, 6; "Jews Tremble at Doorbell, Fear to Answer Telephone," December 22, 1938, 1, 2; "Drive on Jews Gives Germany New Problems," December 26, 1938, 1; "Viennese Restless, Unhappy, Resent Ruthless Nazi Rule," December 28, 1938, 2; "Clamor Rises for Railway Segregation," December 28, 1938, 13; "British Speed Child Exodus from Germany," December 29, 1938, 1; "British Favors to Reich Hinge on Jew Relief," January 4, 1939, 4.

60 George A. Drew (1894–1973), educated at Upper Canada College, University of Toronto, and Osgoode. He became leader of Ontario Conservative Party in 1938, and started a Conservative dynasty in Ontario that lasted forty-two years. He was premier from 1943–48 and went on to become the federal Conservative leader. He was the first chancellor of the University of Guelph and held that role from 1965 to 1971.

61 "Finds Germany Touches Peak of Efficiency," *Globe and Mail*, August 16, 1937, 1.

62 Ibid., 1, 3.

NOTES

63 "Capable of Governing: Like Entering New World to Return from Continent,"
   Globe and Mail, August 19, 1937, 3.
64 "The Facts about Sovietism," August 19, 1937, 6.
65 George A. Drew, "Germany Prepares for Conquest," *The Empire Club of Canada Speeches, 1935–1936* (Toronto: Empire Club of Canada, 1936), 75–91.
66 "War Danger Is Lessening, Claims Drew," *Globe and Mail*, September 11, 1937, 1.
67 William E. Dodd (1869–1940) was born in North Carolina. He was educated at the University of Leipzig and so probably spoke German well. He became a professor of history at the University of Chicago. He was American ambassador to Germany from 1933 until the end of 1937. His daughter, Martha Dodd, wrote extensively about life in Germany in the 1930s. She died in 1990.
68 "Hitler Has Killed More Than Charles II, Claim," *Globe and Mail*, January 14, 1938, 2.
69 "Nazi Envoy Told Speech Free in U.S.," *Globe and Mail*, January 15, 1938, 1.

Notes to Chapter 3

1 He lost his leg in the First World War.
2 Translated as something; none; nothing.
3 Two; three.
4 It seems in fact that this was what Wegenast often did as a child. There are pictures of him dressed for parade, with a musical instrument.
5 On April 5, 1938, Hitler spoke at Innsbruck. Translated into English, he stated, "There had never been any separate mission for Austria: there could never be such a separate mission for any German country. Only one mission could be recognized: to form a single people and to live in a single Reich.... How could folk be so infatuated as to think that a whole people could remain blind to the rise of Germany and on the other hand how could they imagine that I should be blind or deaf to the sufferings of this land? ... I have shared all the sufferings which my homeland had to endure. [On April 10] the whole world will know: on March 13 a man unified a people—a month later the people approved the man.... My fairest work is that I have joined this country, my homeland, to the German fatherland and fairer still that I could restore seven million people to the Reich.... My success may not be approved abroad, but this leaves me unmoved. I can appeal to my people when I wish to consult them and do not have to glue Parliamentary majorities together as each case arises." N.H. Baynes, ed., trans., *The Speeches of Adolph Hitler, April 1922–August 1939* (London: Oxford University Press, 1942), 1453–54.
6 Robert Borden was the prime minister of Canada during the First World War.
7 Martin Niemöller's fate was of wide concern outside Germany throughout 1937 and 1938.
8 Kurt von Schuschnigg, Chancellor of Austria, tried to stand up to Hitler against the Anschluss but failed. He resigned on March 11, 1938, and was imprisoned for seventeen months before being moved to Dachau and later Sachsenhausen. He survived the war.
9 A man Wegenast had met in order to exchange money the day of Hitler's speech.
10 Foreigner.
11 He gave them a ride by letting them stand on the running boards of the car.

12 Canadian Conservative Prime Minister. Wegenast was an ardent Liberal.

13 This is but one example of the details that Wegenast recorded of what was going on around him. He commented several times on the state of poultry farming in Europe.

14 See note 40 from chapter 2.

15 Wegenast makes it clear in this case that he interjected this passage much later.

16 See note 39 from chapter 2.

17 Stendhal was the pen name of the nineteenth-century French writer Marie-Henri Beyle (1783–1842). Well known for his novels, in particular *The Red and the Black*, Stendhal also wrote a great deal of travel literature, in which he described architecture, among other things. One of his best-known books of this genre was *Travels in the South of France*, published in 1838. Wegenast had Stendhal's *Mémoires d'un touriste* with him and found it interesting that Stendhal covered much of the same territory in 1838 that Wegenast covered in 1938.

18 Wegenast does not say what was wrong with his earlier impressions.

19 Virtually on the German border.

20 A town inside Germany but near the Luxembourg border.

21 Near the city of Bonn. Both the Rhineland-Palatinate and Baden-Württemberg are near France, Luxembourg, and the Netherlands.

22 Countries outside Germany.

23 Good morning.

24 These comments on poultry conditions are interesting when compared to rapid developments taking place in the North American chicken situation. Here the Barred Plymouth Rock and the Single Comb White Leghorn predominated. Specialized poultry farms, while not numerous, did exist and in increasing numbers.

25 It is unclear what was contained in this "memorandum." It seemed to be a document that contained information on his heart condition and hypertension, and also the research he had done into the medical implications of bathing cures. He later listed the material he had read on the subject.

26 There is no evidence from the diary that Wegenast took the baths, or that the doctors at Bad Nauheim helped solve his heart problems. He seemed more interested in collecting information than on treatment. Bad Nauheim is still a centre for cardiac research, but faith in CO_2 balneotherapy, a form of hydrotherapy or use of baths for health reasons, is not as strong as it was in the 1930s. Recent studies on the beneficial effects of balneotherapy show mixed results. There is evidence, though, that CO_2 balneotherapy should not be used for severe hypertension or in the case of new cardiac infarctions, or heart attacks. Since Wegenast suffered from both these problems, it would seem that bathing cures in the waters of Bad Nauheim were contradicted in his case.

27 It became known by May 1938 that Hitler planned to invade Czechoslovakia. The Sudetenland elections, with campaigns between March and September, created much tension over how much support (and whether it was real support) would go to the Nazis.

28 Inevitable.

29 See note 39 from chapter 2.

30 Rosenberg, *The Myth of the Twentieth Century*, published in Munich in 1930 as *Der Mythus des 20 Jahrhunderts*. It had sold a million copies by 1944 (with heavy sales promotional efforts), but seemed to have had little political impact

other than as a reinforcing form of propaganda. It articulated the philosophy of the Nazis. It is almost certain that Wegenast read the book in German.

31 Alfred Rosenberg was an early member of the Nazi party. He set out the racial theories of the Nazis with Aryans as a master race, and with strong anti-Jewish sentiments. He believed in the Lebensraum, and argued for the "religion of the blood." His theories were derived from the Englishman/turned Nazi, Houston Stewart Chamberlain, and from the nineteenth-century völkisch movement. Although touted as an important intellectual, his influence on Nazism seemed to be marginal. Most Nazis could not understand the tangled language. Hitler called it nonsense or "rubbish." He considered Rosenberg as weak and ineffectual. Rosenberg was executed for war crimes in 1946 as a result of the Nuremberg war trials.

32 Wegenast's wording of Rosenberg's thought might seem convoluted and nearly incomprehensible, but the reality is that the book was so irrational that it made no sense.

33 Means ethical life and comes from Hegel's teaching. Ethical norms that arise from the interaction of one's own ethical views with those objective values present in structures of society. When these cleave together a person is free.

34 He found the language difficult to understand in any detail, and therefore he sought to sense some generalized meaning behind Rosenberg's philosophy.

35 In preparation for the Olympic Games to be held in Berlin in summer 1936, the Reich began to repress open Jew baiting early that year. This soft-pedalling of anti-Semitic activity encouraged several thousand German Jews, who had left shortly after 1933, to return. Moves by the French government in 1934 to restrict the capacity of foreigners to gain employment in France, because of the severity of the depression, further encouraged German Jews living in France to go back to Germany. By early 1938, at about the time Wegenast was in Germany, the situation had reversed itself. Determined and vicious persecution of Jews had radically escalated. See R. Evans, *The Third Reich in Power* (New York: Penguin Books, 2005), 570–77.

36 This picture has not survived.

37 Dr. Herkel was a doctor that Wegenast met at Bad Nauheim in relation to the water/bath treatments for heart disease.

38 Thin, finely twisted thread.

39 The French article in the *La Republique*, June 4, 1938, contained information on the increasing concern over the Czech problem and over Germany's demand for a return of colonies. Chamberlain was arming and at the same time trying to reach an agreement with the Reich over the Czech issue, and also to settle the problems in Spain and between Spain and Italy. The problem was that there are two totally different stances between totalitarian states and the democracies. Totalitarian states ruthlessly grabbed what they want, and their philosophic thinking was diametrically opposed to that of the democracies.

40 Although he was fluent in both French and German, Wegenast went to some effort to make these documents as accurate as possible. He obviously wanted to be completely clear conceptually in this communication with Lichti. Wegenast did not want to hurt the man personally.

41 The letters were all translated from the original German by Donald Bruce and Christine McWebb.

Notes to Chapter 4

1 This photograph has not survived.
2 This letter has not survived.
3 "One and the same."
4 Pitiful.
5 Temptation.
6 Inevitable, unavoidable, inescapable, necessary.
7 The first correct and full, non-abridged English version of this book, translated by James Murphy, did not come out until 1939.
8 Julius Streicher was the publisher of *Der Stürmer*, which he founded in 1923. The journal poured out anti-Semitic material. Streicher also published three anti-Semitic books for children. He was executed in 1946 as a result of the Nuremberg trials. Goebbels, Hitler's propaganda minister, committed suicide with Hitler. Rosenberg, like Streicher, was executed.
9 Scotland did not have an ancient parliament. See H. Trevor-Roper, *The Invention of Scotland: Myth and History* (New Haven: Yale University Press, 2008).
10 Populist movement with a romantic focus on folklore. Myth. Developed in the nineteenth century, a movement that combined sentimental patriotism, folklore, back-to-the-land; ethnic nationality, anti-Semitic in outlook.
11 A strong example of Wegenast's biased views on British culture.
12 He adhered here to the German author Stoye's thesis, set out in *The British Empire*.
13 *Verteidigen* means "to defend."
14 Humane, decent.

Notes to Chapter 5

1 O. Lubrich, ed., *Travels in the Reich*, 89.
2 The *Globe and Mail* announced that Hitler would edit *Mein Kampf* in order to make it less offensive to the French. The book was to undergo what the Germans called a "historic correction" ("Hitler Edits Mein Kampf to Soothe French Fears," *Globe and Mail*, December 3, 1938, 1).
3 Wegenast's diary, August 7, 1938.
4 P. Fritzsche, *Life and Death in the Third Reich* (London: Belknap Press of Harvard University Press, 2008), 9.
5 Stoye, *The British Empire: Its Structure and Its Problems*.
6 A good source on racism and its relationship to Nazi political thinking can be found in L. Waddington, *Hitler's Crusade: Bolshevism and the Myth of the International Jewish Conspiracy* (New York: Tauris Academic Studies, 2007).
7 See H. Trevor-Roper, *The Invention of Scotland: Myth and History* (New Haven: Yale University Press, 2008).
8 I. Kershaw, *Hitler, Germans, and the Final Solution* (New Haven: Yale University Press, 2008), 6, 120–21.
9 See, for example, R.J. Evans, *The Third Reich in Power* (New York: Penguin Press, 2005), 333–35.
10 See chapter 2, pages 16–17, for reports on Stoye's work in the *Globe and Mail*, which Wegenast must have read.
11 P. Fritzsche, *Life and Death in the Third Reich*, 4, 6, 17.

NOTES

12 Victor Klemperer, *I Will Bear Witness,* volume 1, 165.

13 Ibid., 214.

14 Ibid., 224.

15 Ibid., 229.

16 Ibid., 233–34.

17 Irène Némirovsky, *All Our Worldly Goods*, trans. Sandra Smith (London: Chatto and Windus, 2008), 137 (originally published in French in 1947).

18 "Hitler Edits Mein Kampf to Soothe French Fears," *Globe and Mail*, December 3, 1938, 1.

19 "Berlin Warns Democracies," *Globe and Mail*, December 3, 1938, 3.

20 "International Terror and Intimidation Seen in Nazi War on Jews," *Globe and Mail*, December 19, 1938, 3.

21 "Now Exploiting Torture," *Globe and Mail*, December 20, 1938, 6.

22 "Further Violence Seen as Sequel to Hitler's Victory at Munich," *Globe and Mail*, December 23, 1938, 1, 2.

23 One of the best sources for German opinion is I. Kershaw, *Hitler, the Germans, and the Final Solution* (New Haven: Yale University Press, 2008).

24 Schmidt to Wegenast, December 26, 1938.

SELECTED BIBLIOGRAPHY

Augustine, Ham. Kaufman family fonds. [1877?]–1990. Archives, University of Waterloo Library.

Bessel, R. *Life in the Third Reich*. Oxford: Oxford University Press, 2001.

Diary and Papers of Franklin Wellington Wegenast. Wegenast Family Papers, Private Collection.

Dorothea Palmer Collection. Archives, University of Waterloo Library.

Evans, R.J. *The Third Reich in Power, 1933–1939*. New York: Penguin Press, 2005.

Fritzsche, P. *Life and Death in the Third Reich*. London: Belknap Press of Harvard University Press, 2008.

Gannon, F.R. *The British Press and Germany, 1936–1939*. Oxford: Clarendon Press, 1971.

Gellately, R. *Backing Hitler: Consent and Coercion in Nazi Germany*. Oxford: Oxford University Press, 2001.

Hayes, G. *Waterloo County: An Illustrated History*. Waterloo, ON: Waterloo Historical Society, 1997.

Hitler, A. *Mein Kampf*. Translated by James Murphy. London: Hutchison & Co./ Hurst & Blackett, 1939. Online at http://greatwar.nl/books/meinkampf/.

Kershaw, I. *Hitler*. London: Allan Lane, 2008.

———. *Hitler, the Germans, and the Final Solution*. New Haven: Yale University Press, 2008.

———. *The Nazi Dictatorship: Problems and Perspectives of Interpretation*, fourth edition. London: Arnold, 2000.

Klemperer, Victor. *I Will Bear Witness, 1933–1941: A Diary of the Nazi Years*, volume 1. Translated by Martin Chalmers. New York: Modern Library, 1999.

Koonz, C. *The Nazi Conscience*. London: Belknap Press of Harvard University Press, 2003.

Leibbrandt, G. *Little Paradise: The Saga of the German Canadians of Waterloo, 1800–1975*. Kitchener, ON: Allprint, 1980.

Lubrich, O., ed. *Travels in the Reich, 1933–1945: Foreign Authors Report from Germany.* Translated by Kenneth Northcott, Sonia Wichmann, and Dean Krouk. Chicago: University of Chicago Press, 2010.

Margaret Hyndman Tapes. Ontario Archives. July 1983.

McLaren, A. *Our Master Race: Eugenics in Canada, 1885–1945.* Toronto: McClelland and Stewart, 1990.

Parents' Information Bureau fonds. 1930–1976. Archives, University of Waterloo Library.

Remak, J., ed. *The Nazi Years: A Documentary History.* Englewood Cliffs, NJ: Prentice-Hall, 1969.

Waddington, L. *Hitler's Crusade: Bolshevism and the Myth of the International Jewish Conspiracy.* New York: Tauris Academic Studies, 2007.

INDEX